Very Big Journey

Readers of this work should be aware that if members of some Aboriginal communities see the names or images of the deceased, particularly their relatives, they may be distressed. Before using this work in such communities, readers should establish the wishes of senior members and take their advice on appropriate procedures and safeguards to be adopted.

Very Big Journey

My Life As I Remember It

Hilda Jarman Muir

Aboriginal Studies Press

First published in 2004
Reprinted 2010, 2011
Aboriginal Studies Press
for the Australian Institute of Aboriginal and Torres Strait Islander Studies, GPO Box 553,
Canberra ACT 2601

The views in this publication are those of the authors andnot necessarily those of the
Australian Institute of Aboriginal and Torres Strait Islander Studies.

The publisher has made every effort to contact copyright owners for permission to use
material reproduced in this book. If your material has been used inadvertently without
permission, please contact the publisher immediately.

© Hilda Muir, 2004

Apart from any fair dealing for the purpose of private study, research, criticism or review,
as permitted under the Copyright Act, no part of this publication may be reproduced by
any process whatsoever without the written permission of the publisher.

National Library of Australia Cataloguing-In-Publication Data:

>   Muir, Hilda Jarman .
>   Very big journey : my life as I remember it.
>
>   ISBN 0 85575 397 8.
>
>   1. Muir, Hilda Jarman. 2. Aborigines, Australian - Women -
>   Northern Territory - Biography. 3. Aborigines, Australian -
>   Removal. I. Australian Institute of Aboriginal and Torres
>   Strait Islander Studies. II. Title.
>
>   994.2904092

 This project has been assisted by the Commonwealth Government through
the Australia Council, its arts funding and advisory body.

Cover Photograph by Sue Wicks
Cover Design and layout by Fat Arts
Editorial work by Melissa Lucashenko and Felicia Fletcher
Produced by Aboriginal Studies Press

Contents

Foreword	vii
Preface	ix
Acknowledgements	xi

Chapter 1	White people's ears not too good	1
Chapter 2	Going hunting	11
Chapter 3	Not thinking about colour	16
Chapter 4	Killing on Vanderlin Island	29
Chapter 5	Always hungry	44
Chapter 6	Ringbarking trees	53
Chapter 7	Feeling human	62
Chapter 8	The Big Smoke	74
Chapter 9	Back to Darwin	83
Chapter 10	Flaming furies at Parap Camp	90
Chapter 11	Cyclone Tracy – Floorboards lifting	97
Chaper 12	Nerve trouble	108
Chapter 13	Hilda – World Traveller	118
Chapter 14	Time For change, right now	129
Chapter 15	Kidnapped back home	140
Postscript : The apology		154
Conversion table		156

Arafura Sea
Darwin
Sturt Highway
Katherine
Groote Eylandt
Gulf of Carpentaria
Northern Territory
Borroloola
N
100
km
Stuart Highway
Darwin
Northern Territory

Hilda's country, Wuyaliya clan
Hilda's mother's country, Rrumburriya clan
Muluwa
Wanarrijila
Ngawulunda
Yiyinbinda
North Island
West Island
Bing Bong
Mamarla
Centre Island
South West Island
Vanderlin Island
Mingara Lagoon
Kangaroo Island
Yukuyi
McArthur River
Manangoora
To Borroloola

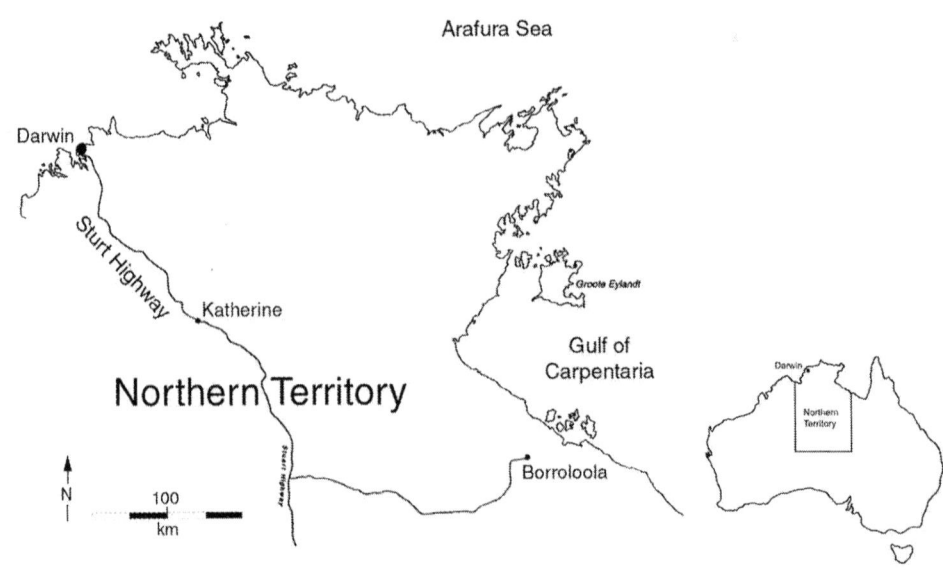

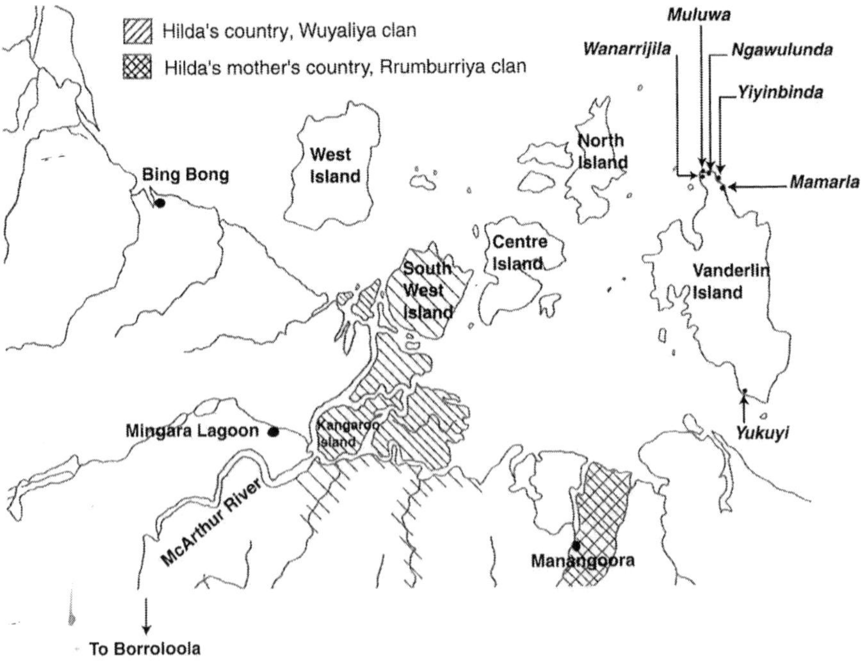

Foreword

This is the life story of Hilda, who journeyed as a young child from her country in Borroloola to the newly established town of Darwin. The journey was on horseback, and her cultural ties and the bond to her mother were severed, forever. Hilda was like many children brought to someone else's country as a result of the stolen generation policies. She survived the hardships of growing up and raising a large family, and a husband who volunteered for World War Two and on return was, like many soldiers, an angry personality when 'on the hops'. He was also a man full of charm and wit. He died during Cyclone Tracy which devastated Darwin in 1974. I became closely attached to Hilda during the mid-1970s when her daughter Cissie and I, along with our children, dared to enter tertiary education in Adelaide. Hilda, depressed after the cyclone, was soon to rise again. She became fascinated with all spheres of the arts and took advantage of her many trips to Adelaide to visit the theatres. NAIDOC in Adelaide was always special for Hilda; to join in the marches, attend the speeches, and then dress up for the Nunga Ball.

Hilda had been a very depressed widow at first — a woman who had been totally dependent on her lifelong partner to be there always. But Hilda has grown as a result of her hard times. Now in her eighties she is younger than ever. When I started to do research for a book which included Hilda's background it stimulated many reflections and much questioning. For Hilda, the discussion of the 'stolen generation story' nationally gave her impetus. She was adamant she wanted to tell her story for her children, but also have a published version for the mainstream community. An application was made to the Aboriginal Arts Board for a grant to cover expenses. A recruit was needed; someone who would assist Hilda and she chose an old mate in Adelaide. Both travelled to Borroloola and other significant places in the Top End. At a later date the manuscript was assisted by

Melissa Lucashenko with the advice and assistance of Jackie Huggins from AIATSIS. A manuscript was created and is now ready for publication. A great achievement. Congratulations Hilda!

Barbara Cummings
ATSIC Chairperson
Darwin
June, 2003

Preface

Hilda Muir was born at Manangoora, near the small outback town of Borroloola in about 1920. It was an era of pearl luggers and bullock drays, and, as a child, Hilda heard graphic first-hand accounts about the dangers of wild white men and their guns. For the Yanyuwa people, the sound of shooting still resonated through their homelands, which were only then coming under the firm control of white authorities. Hilda was born, in other words, on the very frontier of modern Australia.

Hilda's early life was spent roaming the Gulf Country on foot, hunting and gathering bush foods for sustenance, as her people had done for millennia. Her mother was a Yanyuwa person, and therefore so was Hilda, who was known to the clan as 'Jarman'. It mattered little that her father was an unknown white man. This small girl had a name, a loving family, and a secure Aboriginal identity. Under the policies of the day, though, Hilda was removed by the Borroloola police at eight years of age to the Kahlin Home for 'half-caste' children in Darwin. She would never see her mother again. Like other children of mixed Aboriginal/white or Aboriginal/Asian descent, Hilda was deemed more intelligent and more capable than her 'full blood' Aboriginal relations. Children of mixed-race were then seen as tragic but teachable. They were removed, institutionalised, trained for manual labour, and usually sent into white society with few skills and fewer prospects.

Hilda survived the experiences of the Kahlin Home. As an adult she fled the Japanese bombing of Darwin, lived through Cyclone Tracy, and bore ten children to a beloved husband. She discovered the excitements of city living, and became addicted to overseas travel. As an old lady, in 1995 she presented the High Court of Australia with a writ on behalf of her fellow stolen generations children, asserting that the government removals of mixed-race children had been not only immoral, but illegal. Most momentous of all in Hilda's own eyes, in 2000 she finally went home to her Yanyuwa land and was recognised by her own people as a jungkayi: an owner and custodian of that country. This is the story of Hilda's bush childhood, and of her removal from a family who had always claimed her and loved her. It is a story of how institutions can exert a terrible power over the children who inhabit them. It is also the story of how the twentieth-century policy of assimilation failed. Hilda married another 'half-caste' Aborigine, William Daniel Muir. Today Hilda Muir, her Aboriginal children, their children, and those children's children are all living reminders that governments cannot always shape human lives in the ways they might wish. The book has been written in language which can be read and understood by the stolen children themselves. Words such as 'fullblood' and 'half-caste', though considered offensive by many Aboriginal people today, have been used because of the need for historical accuracy.

Melissa Lucashenko
June, 2003

Acknowledgements

I would like to acknowledge the Aboriginal Arts Board for their patience and goodwill, as well as for the funding they provided to the project. Dr John Bradley played a special part in the story, as explained in the last chapter. Thanks to all my Kahlin 'family'. Special thanks to all my children — Cecilia, Harold, William, James, Robert, Jeanie, Patrick, Alan, Thomas and Isabel — who all played some part in the creation of this book. I need to especially thank Cissie, who instigated the process, and was the backbone of the whole project. A big thanks to Barbara Cummings, Isaac Brown and the Darwin community in general for all their encouragement and guidance. Thank you to Tony Roberts for his general support and especially for the Borroloola photos. Thank you to the Northern Territory Archives for access to information and other help. And finally thank you to Jackie Huggins who assisted in getting this book to print.

I am indebted to all these people from the very beginning who have enabled me to step back and reflect on all the good and bad times in my life. I hope you enjoy my story.

A special thanks to Barbara James and Francis Good who had an interest in recording my life stories for safe-keeping in the Library.

Hilda Jarman Muir
June, 2003

Hilda and Billy Muir's family

Darwin
Cecilia   1936
Harold   1939   (deceased)
William   1941

Brisbane
James   1944
Robert   1946   (deceased)

Darwin
Jeanie   1947
Patrick   1948   (deceased)
Alan   1949
Thomas   1951
Isabel (Muki)   1952

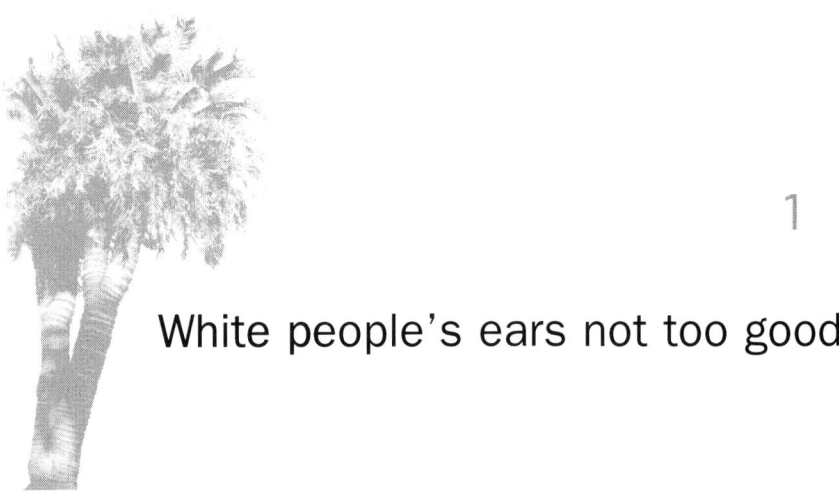

1
White people's ears not too good

I am writing this story because I wish to tell my dear children and their children of my life from my early childhood. When I'm gone it may remind them of who their ancestors are, and their true Yanyuwa identity.

Official records show I was born on 26 January 1920. I used to think I was born at Borroloola, but when I went back there nearly fifty years later, my countrymen told me I was born at Manankurra (or Manangoora as I remember it), on the Wearyan River. My birth was a proper bush birth in our country, near Manankurra. Being born in the bush meant that the exact year and month of my birth was never registered. My official birthday was given to me when I went to Darwin and the authorities registered me. They decided that the date of Australia Day — 26th January would be good enough and guessed my year of birth to have been 1920.

Manunkurra is about sixty kilometres or two days by foot from Borroloola. By water, it's about 160 kilometres or three days by canoe down the McArthur River from Borroloola and then along the coast in the Gulf. Manankurra was spelt 'Manangoora' when a pastoral lease was taken out on our old Yanyuwa ceremonial grounds.

My mother was a full blood Yanyuwa woman with the traditional name a-Manankurrmara. White people called her Polly. My father was a white man but he never claimed me, so I do not know who he was. By the time I wanted to know about my father, my mother was dead.

I was called Jarman by my Yanyuwa people. Perhaps this was the Yanyuwa way of saying 'German' as my father may have been German — there were some German people around the Gulf country in those days. When I went back to Borroloola I was still known by the old people as Jarman. Years later, in 1948, when I was grown up, married and living in Darwin, I heard that an old man, Paddy Doran, was looking for me and telling people that he was my father. Paddy was working for the railways at the Twenty-two Mile and claiming me as his daughter. The McGinnesses, Barney and Carrie's family, contacted me and told me Old Doran was trying to trace his girl Hilda from Borroloola. He said he was my father and had named me Hilda when I was born, but had not given me his surname. When I used to think back I could get quite angry about how I couldn't trace my father because I didn't know his name — then all those years later this man was trying to get in touch with me and was telling me that he was in Borroloola when I was born and had named me Hilda, but had not given me a surname. I couldn't make out whether he really was my father. It just didn't feel right, because if he was, my people would not have called me Jarman.

When Ray Bridgland, the Borroloola policeman wrote my name down, he got it wrong too. He wrote my name down as Hilda Narma. It never was Narma! It seems like he just didn't listen properly. It's Jarman, not Narma as the Borroloola police records show. Now when I've begun putting my story down for my family and their families, I've heard that someone has found out my 'bush' name. It seems that Yulama was what my kin called me when I was little — Yulama. It took me long enough to find my family name — sixty years is a pretty long time, but it was better to find out before I finished the book than afterwards. I also found out that my Yanyuwa name is a-Marrayimara.

So, the old Borroloola policeman, Bridgland, heard Jarman or Yulama as Narma. It seems white people's ears are not too good. They never got Aboriginal names right. In those days my people didn't care about those things. They didn't know what the police or welfare people were writing about because that was something only for them to see. Only the whites want to write everything down, measure everything, count everything. How far, how long, how many, as if that makes it better, or different or something. Well count, measure, or write, it doesn't change the fact that Hilda Yulama, daughter of a-Manankurrmara, is safe as an old woman now, with her Yanyuwa name, a-Marrayimara and family name, Yulama.

When I learnt that the name from my mother's country is a-Marrayimara, I was also told that my mother was married in a proper marriage, a real law marriage, to an old Yanyuwa man. The only thing was that he wasn't there with Mum all the time. Maybe that's why I don't remember him. I'm light-skinned which is why I think my father was a white man.

In those days, because I had a white father and an Aboriginal mother, I was labelled a half-caste. Of course nowadays every half-caste person is considered Aboriginal, but in the old days, white people loved to give everyone a tag so they could put us here or there, depending on how white or black they thought we were — like cutting out sheep or cattle, this one that way and that one this way, herding us into one yard or another, depending on which gate they opened and which gate they slammed shut. So you might be half-caste, half-and-half, or you might be quadroon, which was a half-caste mother (usually) and a white father. Then they had octoroon and I reckon you had to have pretty good eyes or know something to say someone is octoroon which meant someone with a quadroon mother and a white father. Sometimes it was the other way around but it nevertheless meant you were pretty white-looking. All of these labels just depended on how the official saw you, whether he thought you were very light or very dark. It was up to the individual, like so many decisions that were made on our behalf. Whether we got labelled half-caste or quadroon wasn't decided through an official asking who your mother, father or your grandparents were. It just depended on what the official thought he saw when he first looked at you. It didn't make any difference to us Yanyuwa mob what the whites, the welfare and the police reckoned and wrote down in their long, ruled books. We lived with our mothers and relations the way all our generations had for thousands of years — hundreds of generations. I didn't know any half-caste kids when I was living with my mother and our people. We were all Yanyuwa.

    I lived in the Malarndarri camp across the river from Borroloola and I remember clearly those early eight years. There were lots of little kids running around quite happily climbing trees, chasing, going bush and hunting with their mothers, sisters and aunties for food — goanna, sugar-bag (bush honey), plums, and berries when they were in season, and yams. There were always yams all year round.

    Living off the land meant we were always going from one place to another. We followed the food in season. My people had a good variety of food all year. We travelled around the coast onto Vanderlin Island where there was always plenty of fish, turtle and dugong. We also went fishing on the McArthur River, the Robinson River, and the sea gulf around Vanderlin Island. We also looked for other bush foods in the dry country round Borroloola, Bing Bong, Batten Point and McArthur River. That's very rich country.

    The richest place was where I was born at Manankurra, my mother's Tiger Shark Dreaming place on the Wearyan River. At this place all the great cycads were brought by the tiger shark from the East. This is the most sacred place — the Cycad Dreaming, the real centre of our country, the eye, the heart. The important Yam Dreaming place is near there and there was a big fresh water well there too.

For generations my people collected salt to put on dugong to keep it for eating later — the same as white people salted beef. Later on Horace Foster and Bill Harney got salt from the big salt pan near here to send it away in bags on boats to Burketown and Darwin. Yanyuwa people, men and women, worked there for Horace Foster. When Harney and Foster came to Manankurra, my people lived as they always had in the old days. The only difference now was that those two white men bagged the salt and sold what the Yanyuwa scraped and heaped. My people were happy working there. It was like the old days when they did it for their own use. There was still plenty of food and plenty of water and it was a big ceremony place too.

This was a big place for Yanyuwa ceremonies. Rich country is good for hunting and plenty of food meant that big mobs of people could gather for ceremonies. Our country covered all the land near the McArthur River mouth, the lower parts along the Wearyan, across the sea to the Sir Edward Pellew Group of islands, Vanderlin Island and all those places. The Yanyuwa called all this country Ma-Wirla, which means a place where there is a lot of food so that many people can get together and use it. There was always food and sweet water there. There was plenty of food like cycad nuts, dugong, sea turtle, sea turtle eggs, fish, shellfish and crabs. On our land we found long-necked turtles, wallaby, kangaroo, goanna, lizard, snake, wild honey, wild vegetables, fruits and yams.

Cycad nuts grow in a bunch on cycad palm trees but they're very poisonous. The Aboriginal people broke the hard shell on the outside, picked the outer skin and sliced it like a potato. They took it to a creek and let it soak for a week. After that they let it dry for a day or so and then all the poison would be gone. You can throw it on the coals to cook, or grind it and make flour for damper and wrap the damper in paperbark and cook it on the coals. Sometimes people kept dried nut slices for grinding and people leaving Manangoora could take the dry cycad food with them. There was salted dugong, too, which was good food to keep for travelling.

Although I was very young, this early bush life stands very clearly in flashes in my mind. I remember some of the places where my mother and my relatives went and what we did. They had knowledge of the land and the old people could read it the way we read books nowadays. They knew the bush: what was good to eat and what was poisonous, where to find water in the ground or which trees to use to wet your mouth. They had this amazing intelligence about the land, God's gift to them for survival in the desert and semi-desert country. I don't know if the early Europeans would have had this intelligent understanding. Maybe Aboriginal people today are losing it too. But Yanyuwa are very clever people to be able to live in bush country.

As a bush child, my life was happy and carefree and I had all my relatives around. Every day I was learning more about the land and survival, speaking language and being a little Yanyuwa. I was a proper bush child, with my family and my culture. I lost all this when I was taken away. Now I can only survive with a corner shop or supermarket.

One incident I remember clearly was when an Aboriginal man, maybe from another tribe, grabbed my mother in the middle of the night and we ran away with him to another country. Thinking back now I realise I must have been about five or six when this happened. I'm telling the story as I lived it — from what's still in my memory. In Aboriginal law it wouldn't have been safe for him just to come into other people's country and stay there. He had to run away with my mother to keep her. This was like eloping. I think this was the custom — that he would take my mother away and have her for himself. I remember some things very well.

The place we went must have been a tableland, a stony escarpment, and we travelled into desert country. There were hardly any trees but there was lots of spinifex in thick sharp clumps. Maybe we had to travel very far away before he had the right to claim her. I don't know what tribe or country this man came from or how he knew my mother. Maybe he just fell in love. I don't know if there was any courting, all I know is we just woke up in the night and ran away. This man stole my mother at night and we went walkabout to another country.

We travelled through desert country and I remember there was no water. It was very dry and I was thirsty. I remember this next incident very clearly — my mother urinated just to wet my face and lips.

I want to write this part of life down, the part that happened when I was still living with my mother as a bush child, with the customs of our people ensuring our survival. It is so amazing to me now to remember that I lived the life of a Yanuywa. As an old woman living in Darwin now, my life is quite different and it is hard to believe I ever lived with Yanyuwa.

I remember during this long journey we climbed a jump-up, a sort of a cliff or sharp rise in the ground. We jumped or scrambled up, and it was a sort of desert country. We travelled on and on but I don't know for how many days. We had hardly any water and perhaps not even enough food. It's marvellous that we survived in the desert like that. The man used to walk a long way in front, carrying a spear and with a dilly bag hanging around his neck. Mum used to carry our worldly possessions, a swag, billycan, tomahawk, things like that and I'd be walking along with spinifex poking at me and I'd be tired and wouldn't be able to walk any further. She couldn't carry me so I used to sit down and cry and I'd be kicking my legs and gammon taking a fit. Mum would come back and try to pick me up and carry me but I'd put on a turn. The poor old lady used to try to pick me up and carry me with a little bit of a swag on one hip. The man would be a long way ahead and I thought he was a blooming cow. He was a proud-looking man who didn't help carry the belongings, he just carried a spear and a dilly bag around his neck. My poor mother was like a slave. Well, that's how it seems now when I remember following this man across the desert. Back then I didn't think that — it all just seemed natural. But now, thinking back, I feel sad for dear old mother. It makes me sad and stirs up emotions in me that I haven't had for a long time. Writing about this makes it all come back to me but I want to make myself remember so that I can tell my children about my life in those days as a little bush girl, crying and hot, with no water in the desert.

I remember a desert tree, thick and not very big — a water tree with an elbow-shaped branch. Mum cut the elbow with a tomahawk and the water gushed out. We wet our lips and swallowed some because our mouths were dry and hot but the water was bitter, salty and brackish. You have to know where to find water to survive on a bush walkabout. After a lot of walking we came to a homestead with a stockyard next to it and we stayed for a while with some people. Whether they knew us, or the Aboriginal man, I don't know, but I remember them branding cattle. They had big iron rods they put on the fire then they knocked the bullocks over and branded them — young bullocks they were. I can't remember the initial on the branding iron. If I had known that I would know which station we had arrived at. Looking at the map now, I see it could have been Eva Downs. Sometimes I have in my mind that someone said Soudan but I don't know for sure — it's too far back. I remember there was a windmill and a bit of a creek with a little bit of garden there next to the windmill. Watermelon and pumpkin were growing and it was very green. I don't know how long we stayed there before we started travelling again.

We walked through rocks, smooth rocks, on a sort of plateau. It could have been the Arnhemland tableland and that old Aboriginal man, her new husband, was still walking in front of us and we just had to trail behind. Mum probably carried a little billycan with water but it wouldn't have lasted.

We followed a route through the desert where there was no hunting. This was a walking route not a hunting place. The little dry soakage place wasn't like a billabong that dries out where there are lily roots in the ground. These roots are eaten in a similar way to potatoes or beetroot today and lily roots are always there when the billabong dries out — lilies and turtles. Turtles bury themselves when a billabong goes dry but you always know where they are. There's a crack in the ground on top of them — one big crack with lots of little ones around it. When you see this crack you know that turtles are buried deep down in the cool and damp, and you can get them for a feed. But there was nothing like that in the desert, only rocks and spinifex. There was probably goanna for food, but not much of anything else.

I reckon we went from Borroloola across the Barkly Tableland. There was no road or track, it was desert country with no trees, just flat with stones and spinifex and the sunlight hurt our eyes. I don't know how long we travelled from Borroloola, but we just keep going, across plains and spinifex ridges. There were no hills and no creeks.

I can't remember leaving that place but we crossed through a long creek bed and eventually came to Anthony's Lagoon. We stopped there for a short while with some people called Biondi. They were half-castes like me and had white fathers. They lived on the side of the river or creek. To me it looked like a river, a great big lagoon, with high cliffs and we did a little fishing there. The Biondis had little babies that looked like twins and they all welcomed us, and greeted us as if they knew us as family. Next to Anthony's Lagoon, just at the top near the hill, was the police station with a goat yard next to it. Mum went into the police station. She must have spoken a little English, pidgin probably, and she knew how to ask about things. She always used to call into a police station if she wanted to find out anything. She seemed like an incredible woman to me. Maybe we got our rations there. I don't know what year the government started giving out rations but I know that when we asked at the police station for rations we got a twist of black tobacco (niccy), sugar, a small packet of flour and tea leaves.

When we left, we travelled on rocky slabs near the edge of the tableland and then we came to a hill on the creek side. This must have been Walhallow Station. It must have rained because there were pools of water and we camped in a cave. I remember seeing paintings on the walls of the cave, the same as I saw later at

Nourlangie — a figure of a man and something like a kangaroo. The cave was full of what I thought were little birds, but they were bats. At Walhallow we got water and food from the creekbed. The countrymen there put their sweat on my mother and me. They held us and rubbed the sweat from their arms and armpits on us. Maybe they did that before they allowed us to drink the water. It was like they were initiating strangers from another country. They held us like that and then we got to drink some water. It was custom.

When I think back we must have walked a very long way through different places and different country. We survived off the land as we went. I vividly recall eating little cucumber melons.

It's funny what you remember and what you don't, but I know the places where we travelled in daytime, in the light. I remember walking back to Borroloola with Mum, but I can't remember anything about that Aboriginal man and I don't know what happened to him. I do remember that at McArthur Station he wasn't there. Maybe he was a Tableland man and stopped there when we got to where his people were. It's strong in my mind that it was a long walk but there is no one to ask about that now. Those who could tell me are now dead.

2

Going hunting

At McArthur Station there was a chap called Joe Scrutton who was a very tall half-caste man. He had his son, who was just a little boy, with him. In the old days, Old Charles Scrutton was the head stockman for the McArthur River Station. He was probably father to this good looking young fella, Joe Scrutton. The bit of land old Scrutton stocked up is called Bauhinia Downs though sometimes people say Bohemia Downs. This was in the wild times before police came to Borroloola to stop white stockmen shooting Aboriginals — and to stop them shooting one another. They were very wild men, those white men.

Anyway, at McArthur Station we saw Yellow Minnie's daughter, a quadroon girl called Sarah, and we met the Campbell family. The old people, Mr and Mrs Campbell, Pat Turner's grandparents (Pat Turner, a niece of Kumanji Perkins, is a former ATSIC CEO), were camped along the river with their team of horses and their three children. Aunty Katie was the eldest child and there were two boys. We visited them and they greeted us, showering us with little presents of wool and hankies. I don't know if we were related or whether they just welcomed us as their fellow men. I don't know, but that's what happened when you met up with people. They just sort of welcomed you and gave you gifts.

When I was about seven we left McArthur Station and came back to Borroloola, back to our country. That's where my mother belonged and where she wanted to be. The Aboriginal man disappeared from my memory. He disappeared as mysteriously as he had come into our lives that night. He just came and went. Mum and I stayed in the camp on the other side of the river from Borroloola. Malarndarri was the place our people camped in little iron shacks and bark bough shades — not really close to the river, but back a bit, and high, so we could see if anyone was coming from the river. If someone was coming, if we needed to, we could run and hide in the scrub behind the camp.

Malarndarri was now the main camp for the Yanyuwa people from Borroloola. The town was on the other side, across the water. Our only transport was by canoe. I remember luggers with two masts anchored or coming up the river while I was living at the Malarndarri camp. Mr Harney and Mr Foster used them to bring cargo in from Burketown. Bill Harney and Horace Foster used to invite some of our people on board, including women. They used to grog on, you know, and then at about lunchtime the men would end up overboard. Whether they were thrown or not I don't know, but the white men always kept the women. The camp wasn't very far from where the luggers were and all of the kids watched the lugger and the people onboard.

We used canoes to travel up and down the river and caught fish by spear. I remember going in canoes with my relatives. I would sit at the end of the boat and we'd go close to the bank where the big Moreton Bay fig trees grew. These trees were full of lovely sweet fruit that I used to love to pick. They were big trees, with branches growing over the river. They made a lovely shade and under that shade was a good feeding place for fish, especially the barra. The big ones would swim there and feed on the figs as they fell from the tree. The river is a very clear memory for me.

A Yanyuwa man sat at the front of the canoe with a spear in his hand and fished and another man sat at the end of the canoe paddling. The paddler didn't dare make a splashing noise otherwise he'd frighten the fish. This was one way to get food when we lived in Borroloola, but there was another way. The McArthur River is part fresh water and part salt water, depending on the rise and fall of the tide. The other way to catch fish was to cut branches and just when the tide turns, put them across the river. The fish were caught when the tide went out. They flapped and splashed, caught in the branches we put there. This was near Fletcher Creek.

Sometimes I hunted with my relatives and Jessie, my sister. Mum must have been somewhere else then because I wasn't with her all the time. I know that I used to cry because I wanted to be with her but people told me I had to stay and she went off without me. We roamed up to Bing Bong and Batten Point and back down to Robinson River.

At other times my people travelled down to the coast for sea turtle and dugong. When they caught fish, turtle, turtle eggs or dugong there was food for everyone — enough to feed everyone in the camp. No-one was mean or greedy because sharing is a strong tradition with my people. Vanderlin Island was one of my favourite places. Out there where we went in season for food and ceremonies, there were little soldier crabs and we used to chase them — not for eating, just for fun. And we climbed the lovely big mangroves. When the tide was out we could get in the mud to look for big cockles. You could see the top of them sticking through the mud and you'd sort of scoop them and put them on the hot coals, or boil them up in a billycan. This is how I spent my time. I travelled with my mother and relatives, going bush hunting to get food from the Island and along the coast. There was always a tomahawk, billycan and a digging stick. We were never without these implements. Sometimes we caught big spotted native cats to eat, and wallabies. There was a variety of food in the bush in those days, but it was hard because we had to hunt every day to get food. We always had one or two dogs with us to help us catch kangaroo, bandicoot or goanna, and lizards — the blue tongued or frilled neck. Once on a long walkabout, I reckon we killed a few cattle for more meat and people came to share, as is our custom. There were always berries, whatever the season. There was plenty of this kind of bush tucker — sugar-bag (bush honey), and yams, too which are like potatoes. The vines grow around trees and you dig around the tree and collect the yams. If we thought we had enough, we would stop, but the main thing was survival. Of course, we were always near water, beside a billabong or a lagoon, or we followed the rivers around the coast and islands and kept near the soaks and springs. We had to keep near water.

Bush honey can be found in tree trunks and to find it we'd look up into the tree and watch for the sugar-bag bees. They're really little bees. There's a hole in the tree where the bees fly in and out when they're getting pollen from the flowers. They also build nests in ant beds but this is quite rare. The best bush tucker was sugar-bag. When we'd eaten enough we'd put the rest in a container. People use billycans for this now, but when we were young we used a paperbark basket. We diluted the remainder of the sugar-bag to make a drink. If we ate it, it was like having bread — lovely. Part of the sugar bag was wet with the honey and there was a yellow part, like cake. White people call it honeycomb but we called it cake. For other sweet things we could suck the honey from bottlebrush flowers. They were sweet and good if you were thirsty — especially the ones that grow in the swamp land where there is a sort of soakage. Sometimes, even when it looked all dried up, we'd know there was water in the ground. When we came to that spot we kept digging until we found water. These are the times I remember when I was out with my mother and my people.

When we had had enough to eat we returned to the main camp near Borroloola, Malarndarri. We had dogs which my people had trained from puppyhood to be hunters. My people cut the hair from the animals they wanted to hunt, then they burnt the hair and let the dogs smell it to teach them the scent. My sister Jessie, Mum and I were always going hunting. We roamed around Robinson River, the Wearyan, Manankurra and those places, sometimes going by canoe out to the islands along the coast. Vanderlin is the main Island, but we went to the smaller ones too. The Europeans call them South West Island, West Island, Centre Island and North Island. We also went along the coast to Bing Bong and Batten Point too. We travelled all over. This was my early childhood and I loved it. Where we went and who we went with, depended on the seasons and our ceremonies. Our lives depended on those two things.

This is the life my people lived. We didn't have much white man's tucker then but the police handed it out every week, maybe every two weeks. That was when the Welfare law came in. It must have been about 1920. A little bag of flour, a little bag of sugar, nicotine, what we call niccy — you know, sticks of tobacco, three or four long blocks of tobacco — hard black stuff smoked through a clay pipe or chewed. Men sliced bits off but some old women, like Mum, smoked and chewed. The women preferred to chew, sticking it in their mouths. First they put it in the ashes, rolled it and then chewed it. My people loved that nicotine. Right from the early years everyone loved niccy. I remember going with my mother to the police station to get a handout. The law was that the Welfare or Native Affairs had to start looking after Aboriginal people through the police by providing rations.

3

Not thinking about colour

I don't remember playing with any half-caste kids. We didn't say it that way, I just played with my relatives' kids and they were all my kin. We didn't think any of us were different, just a big mob of kids. We weren't thinking, 'I'm not as black as that one there, or this other one,' and I spoke my mother's language. When I lived with my people I spoke the lingo. I was a happy little Aboriginal kid. We just enjoyed life and played, and we were all Yanyuwa. Our mothers all loved us, and our aunties and uncles and nannas too. We were one big loving family and nobody worried us, no matter which side of the river we played. The adults never growled at us. They were loving, kind people, our family. I never knew of my people belting their children when I was a child. There was never any belting, but there was picking up and holding. Maybe there wasn't much to be naughty about or too many rules to break. It was different to now when people own things and live in houses with small little yards. The kids go to school and don't have much to do afterwards except get into trouble. Our lifestyle involved ceremonies and getting food. We lived on animals and lizards for meat and we had lots of fruits like berries — some sweet, some sour, and water-lily bulbs and stems, like celery. We gathered all the different berries and some had seeds like cherries. They grew when the rainy season came and we smashed them up and ate them that way. In that country there's food to survive on all the time, in every season.

When I lived with Grandad Buscilla Damaso, I must have been six, going on seven. He was Grandad Damaso, but we called him Pop. He was a short, small-built man, a very gentle, lovely man. His daughter's name was Mary, and his son was Basil. Later, when he was older, everyone called Basil 'Babe' Damaso. I'd say Mary would have been about eighteen, and Babe about thirteen at the time and they were my first cousins — their mother and my mother were sisters.

Pop Damaso had overseas work contracts for some Asian countries, for example, Manila in the Philippines. The contracts were for the harvesting of sea slug, trepang or bêche de mer. Later in life I came to know that he was a Filipino. I was told that Captain Matthew Flinders came to the Gulf country in the early 1800s and wrote about a man called Pobassa from Sulawesi. Pobassa made big camps on the island at which the trepang that was harvested would be boiled and dried. Along the coast too. The Yanyuwa people traded pearl and turtle shell for tobacco, grog and Macassan canoes which were dugout canoes with a carved prow. Maybe hundreds of years ago we were trading with the Macassans. Pobassa may have been Pop Damaso's great-grandfather. If you look at the map, Sulawesi, Celebes, is not far south of the Philippines.

I wasn't Pop's daughter but he treated me like I was. He was a very kind and caring man. I don't know how many trips he made to Darwin at that time but there was no proper road to Borroloola in those days. There used to be boats travelling up and down from Borroloola to Darwin, and Borroloola to Roper, getting mail and cargo to take back to Darwin. Stores for everyone came by boat, from Queensland, Burketown or Normanton, or Roper Bar from Darwin. They were then taken by dray or packhorse to

Borroloola. The monthly boat came from Burketown to Roper through Doomadgee, Massacre Inlet and Vanderlin Island. Some boats came direct from Darwin to Borroloola and that's how Pop travelled.

He had a house near where we used to play. All the kids ran around the mud flat area, not far from Rocky Creek. We used to get under the rock at Rocky Creek and play there, making a noise. We wanted to be the one making the biggest noise. Cousin Babe had a three-wheeler bike and he was a big, tall, skinny fella, older than me. The little kids ran after him, laughing and yelling, trying to catch him as he rode around the place.

Mary and Babe's mother didn't live with them at this time. I think she had died in Darwin, so my mother worked for Pop Damaso and looked after Mary and Babe as if she was their mother, as if they were her own children. She was their housekeeper and even though I wasn't Pop's daughter he treated me like I was. Cousin Mary was a beautiful young woman with very long hair and I remember my mother combing it. I didn't meet up with Mary again till many years after I was taken. I was nursing at the Darwin Hospital and she came in to have her second child in April 1934. I had just started work in January that year and I'll never forget it because it was the first time I caught up with my beautiful cousin again.

Pop Damaso had a garden with vegetables and big watermelons. The garden was next to a lovely spring and he grew mangoes there too. To this day there are still mango trees there. Perhaps they're some of the old trees, or maybe they're a new lot. I don't know when he first planted them, but I know he was the first man to plant mangoes in Borroloola. When I was with my mother and cousins we used to help Pop in the garden and get those luscious mangoes. They were big, red, lush and beautiful and I have never seen mangoes like that again. I still remember the spring near Pop's house because it was clear, like glass. It was so beautiful there with a small vegetable garden on one side and mangoes on the other. I specially remember the green strong grasses, fine tall grass growing around that spring pool. But when I went back there in 1973 the spring was overgrown with passionfruit vines and pandanus and there was no sign of that lovely clear, sweet pool that I remembered.

My mother had four children then. The first one in the family was a boy and his name was Harry Gore. His father was Captain Gore who had a lugger called the 'Venture'. He gave his name to Harry who was much older than me. I didn't know much about my brother Harry until I was older. This was because Pop Damaso had taken him to Darwin in Captain Mugg's boat and put him into school there a long time before I was born. But the old people used to tell us about who had left. From generation to generation they told you who our family was and who had gone away. They ground that into you. So when I was taken to Darwin I knew I had a brother, Harry, who had gone to school on Bathurst Island before I was born. This is a story my cousin Mary told me.

When Pop Damaso wanted to put me in the mission school the same as Harry, he was refused permission by the police who had control of all half-caste children. I don't know what age I was then. Pop had put Harry in the Catholic school at Garden Point Mission or Bathurst Island Mission. A lot of children were sent to this mission which was served or run by Catholic priests and nuns. From the time Pop wanted to take me to Darwin to school, and was refused, I didn't see the Damaso family again in Borroloola.

Second along in the family was my sister Jessie, a full-blood girl. Then there was another brother, also a full blood, and his name was Henry. As far as I know I was the last in the family — number four. I worked out how old they were by working out what I remembered from those times. So I know Jessie must have been about twelve years older and Henry probably eight years older than me. I can just remember one time out bush with Jessie. Something was happening. I don't know exactly what, but Mum was nursing my sister like a midwife. I think Jessie was having a baby and that it was stillborn. My sister Jessie's dead and gone now.

I reckon Henry was about eight years older than me. He would have been fourteen, maybe fifteen, and I would have been about six or seven when we were in Malarndarri. Some men grabbed him for a ceremonial thing — men's business. It was a big sad occasion. All the old girls were wailing. From what I remember the women used to present the boys to the men and then they'd be wailing and singing and dancing. I remember they painted the young fellas. He was a marked man, this young fella, going for men's business. The elders, whoever was in charge, marked him with red ochre and white paint. When he was grabbed from the camp all the women were yelling, wailing and hitting themselves. I think I might have been a bit sad with that going on. The old girls were wailing as if he'd committed a crime or something.

They took him away for six or eight weeks to a special place where they kept him. They walked him for days. I don't know how long. That was the custom for young men going for business. They had to be really knocked out so that the elders could do the job. I don't know if Henry ate anything, but he was going to be really tired when he got there. That's what the custom, the law, is. That Henry's gone now, dead, like Mum and Jessie.

After the police stopped Pop Damaso taking me to the mission school in Darwin, Mum went to work at the police station. In those days there was a collection of buildings and I remember as a child thinking that the station itself was very big. It had a verandah around it and there were little bark shade houses and a cell next to the main station house. The tracker's quarters were outside the police station fence, next to the horse yards and the goat yard was further away from the main building. There was a pawpaw tree there and the scent of the flowers was really strong. Some smells still remind me of things I thought I'd forgotten. But, oh, the beautiful aroma of the pawpaw tree — and the pawpaws we used to eat.

The policeman stationed at Borroloola at this time was Mr James Harcourt Kelly. He was from Adelaide and he was very tall and lanky. He must have been over six feet and the Aborigines called him Long Kelly. He had a wife who was short and small-built, with fair hair. I remember her because she treated me very well. They had a daughter, Linda, who was sent away to boarding school and came home from school for the holidays. Linda had lovely long fair hair and I thought she was beautiful.

Mum's job was to take the goats out each day. It might have been so that they could exercise or graze. I don't know how far my mother travelled following the goats but I went with her sometimes and when I got tired I cried to be carried. Poor Mum had had enough of me because her job was to tail the goats, watch them and then bring them back in the afternoon. She also milked them. After a bit, when my mother was taking the goats on walkabout, my mother started jacking-up about taking me along because it was too much for her to carry me when I got tired. I don't blame her. It was too much for her, poor lady, to also carry a five or six-year-old — so she got Mrs Kelly to lock me in the prison cell. All the prisoners were out working, so Mrs Kelly locked me in the cell until Mum was out of sight. My memory of those times is still very clear and strong. I remember seeing all the prisoners working in long gangs round Borroloola. They'd be working out in the heat and sun, with chains round their necks and ankles. Borroloola was well known for its Aboriginal chain gangs.

One time, while Mum was still at the police station, the authorities brought sheep to Borroloola. I think they were experimenting to see how the sheep would cope in the heat. I remember one or two rams with huge twisted horns. I don't know how many they had altogether, or what happened to them, but all of a sudden they were gone. They were a big attraction at the time though. We'd all hang around to see these funny animals that looked so different from goats.

I was really sad when Mr and Mrs Harcourt Kelly left Borroloola. They wanted to take me with them to Queensland. They were always kind to me and I don't know for sure where they went, but they were going to put me in a school down south and adopt me. But old Mum wouldn't let me go. Even now I'm not sure why not. Perhaps I was too small. First Pop Damaso couldn't put me in a mission school because he wasn't my father, then I could have been adopted by Harcourt Kelly but my dear old Mum said that I was too little to leave. Later, when I got bigger, Mum had to let me go with Policeman Bridgland to the half-caste home in Darwin. Maybe Mum thought that was better for me because there were a lot of relations going with me. I don't know. Then again, perhaps she thought that Long Kelly would just take me, put me in school and leave me alone, and not adopt me after all. Maybe that was her thinking. The policemen were always telling the old people that we had to go to school — white man's law: all brown-skinned, half-caste and yellow kids had to be taken away from the camp and put into a white school. They said that when you finished school you could come back on holidays, like Linda Kelly. But those of us who were taken never came back. We were sent out to work and the promises weren't kept. They knew we weren't coming back. The authorities lied to Aboriginal people about what was happening to the children they stole. It happened to my relations, even my brother Harry Gore, when Pop Damaso took him. It had happened to Yellow Fannie's two kids earlier. They were never seen at Borroloola again.

I like to tell these stories about my mother because I realise now how incredible she was. After the Kellys left she got another job. We went to the Borroloola pub, the Tattersall's Hotel, which was owned by three Irishmen: Tim O'Shea, Jim O'Keefe and Jim Moriarty. They were all related, cousins or close kin. Jim Moriarty was the father of John Moriarty of Jumbana Designs who painted the planes for Qantas. John's mother, Kathy, was my country-woman. That old pub was the meeting place for everyone who came to Borroloola — station people or travellers passing through or the hawkers who travelled by wagons, or packhorses. Mum was a dairy maid. She milked the cows that supplied the pub with milk. The hotel was a long building up on stumps with bits of tin on top to stop the white ants. It had a wide verandah all around with vines strung between the verandah posts at the front. It was an old pub, not very big, with a couple of steps leading up to the verandah. There was a big tamarind tree in front, fenced-in, and mango trees as well. Another tree I remember was a date palm tree with a big thick trunk and wide-spread fronds. I kept my eye on it because it had big dates on it and Tim Hogan, the publican, used to give me some. But the tamarind tree was where the travellers stopped for drinks before journeying to another area. It was very popular with the men but there were very few women who drank there. Borroloola was a wild place then and the many white men who came there for their different reasons, sat under the trees, perhaps sharing stories of their travels or the folk back home. I know it was a a beaut place to rest and it must have been heaven to sit under it, enjoying company or just a drink and passing the time of day. They had race meetings there, too, in front of the pub. There was no special track. The race was held there with horses flying past in the dirt and dust.

Tim Hogan did most of the work about the place and he was good to me. If he went to the storeroom and I was there, following him, he'd give me a handful of raisins or currants. He would always find something for me, sultanas or biscuits. I used to love watching the butter making. He'd pour milk into a small machine and turn the handle. There were two spouts, one turning out cream, the other one butter. The cream was white and then the butter came out all thick and yellow.

We had all this luxury and we were never short of food. We didn't live in the main house, we lived outside in our little shelter. The hotel's gone now. Somebody said it caught fire and burnt down in about 1956. The old separate kitchen fell down, too, they reckon in about 1977, eaten by white ants. But those two old trees, the tamarind and date palm, are still there. The palm trunk is withered now, bent over with the wear of seventy years, with its dry fronds clinging. The tamarind tree is still strong, but not as big as when I was little. They're much more hardy and don't wear out with the years. They only lose branches, not their green leaves. But that whole area's an awful mess now, covered with rusting refrigerators and car bodies and ugly things that no-one wants. It made me very sad and wild to see it looking like that. People have no respect for history. That mess spoils my memories.

Next to the hotel was a two-storey house. It must have been six feet off the ground. It was a good flash house and it was also a store where you went to buy clothes and the things you get from department stores. Two old men lived on the place, brothers named Cliff and Tom Lynott. They were pioneers in northwest Queensland, out Winton way and they had wagon teams that brought in goods. Tom Lynott was the first manager of the McArthur River Station and before I was born, Cliff Lynott had come to Borroloola and built a house and shop. Then his brother Tom arrived from McArthur and they ran the shop together. They were old men in those days.

I remember playing under the old house and by that time Tom was dead. I'd play with other little kids and we'd hear footsteps up top of us and giggle and say it's old Tom walking round up there. A ghost. We were half laughing and half scared.

Tom Lynott had been very harsh with my countrymen in the early days. The Yanyuwa people were upset at what was happening to their country. They were hunted off the water they'd used for generations. The white fella's cattle messed up the soaks and springs, and fences went up. The Aboriginal people retaliated and old Tom apparently sent out a mob of men to shoot my relatives. These revenge killings happened until the government sent a policeman to Borroloola the next year to keep the peace. My relatives would tell me about these times, the frightening killing times. There were times when they had had to run and hide. Borroloola was a very wild place. Runaway white fellas came there, hiding, and changing their names so the police couldn't find them. It was a very bad place for Yanyuwa people in those days and they were scared of those wild men. The police were sent to stop the whites shooting Aboriginal people and one another.

If Yanyuwa killed one another, it was for real business and the Yanyuwa understood that. But the whites killed for no reason. Then they went to court and were sent to gaol or paid a fine. The Yanyuwa made a film called Two Laws about their people and the law and many of my relations are in it. It tells about a bad policeman at Borroloola in the 1930s who acted like the whites in early days when the old people were alive. They blamed him for what happened to one woman. My people acted out the sad story of that poor woman and the policeman. They showed how he tied her up and gave her no food, only salty water to drink. He belted her a bit, too. Then they showed their sorry business, after she died.

There was a lot of fighting and violence in those days between white and black and my people were often frightened. I remember one man on horseback chasing my family, my countrymen, as if just for the pleasure of seeing them run helter skelter. One time one old man jumped in the water and hid. He was under the water-lilies, under the water. He stuck just his nose out to breathe, hiding from the man with the gun and horse. Then he listened. Once the white man had gone he got up fast and walked away, looking for food. That's what those old fellas, our uncles and aunts, used to tell us as little kids. We knew the stories about the killings. So we were really scared of strange white people.

The Lynott brothers were harsh people, but there was a Chinese man there too, who was better. His name was Chin Kahen but I'm not sure of the spelling. We said Ki Yan or something like that. He had a big market garden just the other side of Rocky Creek, but a long way from the hotel. The town people must have got their vegetables from this Chinese man who lived over near Pop Damaso. We used to go to his house and he was kind to us. He'd play records for us on one of those old gramophones with the trumpet shaped speaker and the music must have been Chinese because it was high pitched and sounded a little jumbled up — a wah-wah sort of noise.

There was one other man worth mentioning who lived not far from Pop Damaso and Ki Yan. This was Mr Charlie Havey, one of the top men in the town. He had something to do with all the government people in Borroloola at the time. He was a highly respected man and a lovely man. He was a Justice of the Peace and the Magistrate — he had the top job. He was also the butcher, the postmaster and the shipping agent. Charlie Havey was a striking man to me — tall and well-built. He was a quiet man and popular with everyone. He had a general store, which wasn't anything flash, just a big iron shed with lots of goods in it: saddles, bridles, whips, boots, everything for people on the land. It was like a hardware store and I remember going there with my mother to buy a billycan and sticks of tobacco and seeing all the things hanging on the wall. He was also the agent for a boat, the 'Leisha', which came and tied up at the mouth of Rocky Creek. He had another boat, a cutter, for delivering freight and moving some of his stuff around. Charlie lived at the store. He had a few goats and fowls and a big vegetable garden watered by the fresh spring, near Rocky Creek. His store often had little chickens as well as full-grown ones running around inside. He kept the tiny ones in there to save them from the big brown kites, the hawks, and they stayed inside when they got bigger. He was a very kind-hearted man, with all those chooks running round in his shop. It didn't stop people going there, though.

His house, with a verandah alongside, faced Rocky Creek. He spent a lot of his time there on a bullock-hide stretcher. You'd see him lying back there, smoking his pipe, drinking tea from an old pannikin and reading his paper — sometimes with a whisky or rum. He seemed a really relaxed man for someone with so much to do in Borroloola. They called him 'Two Bob Charlie' because they reckoned nothing in the shop was under two shillings.

Not far from where Mr Havey lived there was a sort of stockyard or abattoir where he killed bullocks so the people of Borroloola had fresh meat. Charlie held the Bing Bong pastoral lease, but he didn't live there. Some of my countrymen, Aboriginal stockmen, looked after it for him. They had just enough cattle to supply Borroloola. Old Pluto was the head stockman living on Bing Bong who kept an eye on things. I don't know how the meat was delivered because there were no cars. I can only remember bullock dray transport in those days, and packhorses. But there was no rush in those days. Maybe even the flies were slower.

Charlie Havey lived with a Yanyuwa woman, Yama. They didn't have any children but her family reckoned Charlie was a relative in their family. He always seemed to have plenty of Aboriginal people living or staying near his house. It looked like he was the guardian for many Aboriginal people. As a JP, he could help them sometimes, for example Yellow Fannie, a half-caste woman who lived near his place who had three children with her. Bella was eldest, Belberinda was the second, she was about my age, and the youngest was a boy called Owen. I remember Yellow Fannie because I knew her kids. Before she went to live at Charlie Havey's she'd had two other children. The first two were taken away 'for schooling' and, as usual, Yellow Fannie never saw them again. When this happened to her it was a big heartbreak. The same as for everyone, each time. So everyone knew what happened to Timmy Hampton and his sister. They were taken away and never seen again by their mother, Yellow Fannie, or their relatives. So we knew what 'going to school' meant.

Yellow Fannie made up her mind that her next three kids weren't going to vanish like that, stolen from her loving arms. She must have been a very strong and determined woman. She went and saw Charlie Havey and he told her what to do to make sure Belberinda, Bella and Owen, her last brown skin children, weren't taken away. With Charlie Havey JP to help Fannie, those three kids weren't taken, they stayed with her in Borroloola. That's how Yellow Fannie, the half-caste who didn't have any schooling, who was born a long time before the removal of children laws came into being, fought that law and won the right to have her three children stay with her. She beat that law.

Charlie Havey (seated at far right), Jimmy Gibbs (seated second from right), J. H. Kelly (standing fourth from right) and R. R. Bridgland (standing third from right).

Hilda with Rev. Heathcock and Sister Ruth Heathcock, Matron of the Kahlin Half-caste Home, 1932.

Children at the Kahlin Half-caste Home. Darwin 1928.
(Photo courtesy of the Australian Archives exhibition 'Between Two Worlds', 1993)

Young children from the Kahlin Home at Mindil Beach, Empire Day, 1930s.

Ruth Heathcock (former Kahlin Home Matron) left, with Hilda, 1993. (Photo courtesy *Adelaide Advertiser*)

Kahlin Compound 'sisters', reunion. *Left to right*, Daisy Ruddick, Hilda Muir, Ethel Buckle, Daisy Williams, Pearl Graham, Eileen Austral, Evelyn Baird and Susie Markham.

Some of Hilda's Borroloola family. *Left to right*, Eileen McDinny, Connie Bush, Thelma Douglas, (man and woman unknown) Hilda and Carrie McGinness.

Gathering of the Stolen Generation at Kormilda College in Darwin. Hilda is sitting in front at right.

Hilda Muir in her early teens, 1935.
(Photo taken at Stonehouse Studios, Darwin)

Hilda and friends from Kahlin. (*Left to right*) Hilda with baby Cecilia, Sally Grant and Gladys Ah Mat (nee Kruger). (*Sitting*) Maggie May with baby John Mayo.
(Photo taken at Stonehouse Studios)

Hilda and Elizabeth Cubillo (nee Sayles).
(Photo taken at Stonehouse Studios, 1935)

Hilda and Cecilia (aged about 12 months)
at the Labor Day picnic at Adelaide River,
1937.

Cousins Mary and Babe Damaso with Hilda's brother Harry Gore.

Hilda with children (*left to right*) Cecilia, William and Harold in Brisbane, 1943.

Cousin Babe Damaso with wife Nancy and children (*left to right*) Nancy-Anne, John and Cecil.

Hilda's Kahlin 'sister', Bridget Johnson (nee Baird) with her husband John and (*left to right*) John (baby), Shirley and Barbara.

Allie Ah Mat (family friend) and Bill Muir (*right*).

Bill Muir (*front*) with Scully family (*left to right*) Mona, Joseph, Sarah, Frances, Michael (baby) and Gladys.

Cycad tree at Manangoora, near Borroloola.

John Bradley, anthropologist and family friend.

Borroloola River, 2000.

The tamarind tree that stood in front of the Borroloola pub during Hilda's childhood, 1973.

Hilda next to the date palm that was an early childhood landmark, 1973.

4

Killing on Vanderlin Island

In those days we people didn't call people half-caste, we called them yellow, as in Yellow Fannie and Yellow Minnie. Being yellow didn't matter to Aboriginal people, not like it did to the welfare and police when they were taking children away. Aboriginal people just called you 'yellow' meaning your colour was spoilt, not meaning that you didn't belong. That's why Yellow Fannie wanted to keep her children with her. She loved them and they were an important part of her big, wide family. Now that I'm older I wonder why the officials won when Pop Damaso wanted to take me to school. I'm still very sad that Pop wasn't allowed to do that good thing for me, just because I wasn't his blood daughter. But the police didn't win with Yellow Fannie and Charlie Havey; she kept those kids.

It's a pity my Mum and Pop Damasco didn't go and talk to Charlie Havey about Pop putting me into the Darwin mission school. Things might have turned out differently for me. But Pop Damaso couldn't speak strongly on my behalf. His English wasn't too good, so he didn't have the same power. Then in December 1927 a big business happened that changed my whole life.

An Aboriginal man named Gilprey killed two people — a husband and wife, on Vanderlin Island. Some people say they were getting turtle eggs on sacred ground and had transgressed Aboriginal law by walking on sacred ground. The gossip was that Gilprey was after their young daughter, Ida, for his girlfriend. I believe, what other people say — that the people were sung — Ida's mother and father were sung for going on to sacred ground and getting turtle eggs. If you were sung, it had to happen — according to our law you would be killed. But I don't know anymore. Ida must have been seven or eight, like me. She wasn't a very big build — she was only a small thing.

At the time of the murder we were all there, all kin, my mother and Ida's mother and father, roaming around Vanderlin. We were all sisters, brothers and cousins — one family from Manangoora. Was Gilprey after this young girl, Ida? I don't know.

A long time after this happened, I'd been taken to the half-caste home in Darwin, this same Ida, my cousin Ida Hampton Ninganga, told her story to the anthropologist Dr John Bradley. She told him, in Yanyuwa language, what they all reckoned had happened on Vanderlin Island when her father and mother, (my uncle and aunty), were killed. But this time she told of a lot more things than I remember or knew. Ida had stayed with her relatives and they'd kept talking about what had happened, the way families talk about big things like murders. They keep telling the story over and over, getting all the details straight. So Ida probably told Dr John Bradley only a bit of what she remembered, things she kept hearing from her family and repeated over the years. Later, she went back to Vanderlin but I never saw the Island again. What I'm telling you is what I remember from when I was eight and I've never talked about it to anyone until now.

This is Ida Hampton Ninganga's story as it was recorded in the Yanyuwa language in July 1991 by Dr John Bradley. He then translated it, as it's written here. He later sent me a letter with the story because it's my story too, about how we were on Vanderlin and what happened when we were there, how we were then brought to Borroloola by the police, early in 1928.

The Death of My Mother and Father
by Ida Hampton Ninganga

My elder sister her name was a-Jawinjarama, her whitefella name was like mine, Ida. She was with my mother and father when they were killed. They were at Yiyininbinda. My mother's name was a-Aralka and her whitefella name was Melba. My father's name was Jayungurri and his whitefella name was Peter or Friday. We were on Vanderlin Island, not far from Muluwa [Cape Vanderlin]. Also with us was my mother's sister a-Manankurrmara, and her daughter Hilda. I think her name is a-Marryimara. There were others with us too. My father, mother and sister had gone out hunting for the day. My father said to my mother, 'I'm going to go and get some turtle eggs'. My mother and sister were there. They had just made a fire and had got some water, when my mother saw that old man, Gilprey or Walala, running towards her. He ran to my mother and began to hit her, my mother got away and ran, eastwards across the flat country. Gilprey saw her and chased her. But my mother ran quickly and crossed over a creek. So Gilprey got a spear and speared her. The spear went into her chest and came out near her armpit. My mother, the poor thing, pulled the spear out and kept running. She rested and tied her arm up with a rag. My sister she had hidden herself away in the scrub when that old man had come. My father was still there in the north gathering turtle eggs. Gilprey Walala had left my Mother because she had died. He just left her there. Gilprey went north to Mamarla looking for my Father. He saw him in the distance, so he climbed a tree to wait for my Father. My Father came bearing with him a paperbark bundle of turtle eggs. Gilprey speared him. From the tree he threw the spear. He speared my Father in the thigh and my Father fell. Gilprey climbed down from the tree and hit him until he died. Gilprey then dragged my Father and hid him. We never found his body. Nobody ever found it. Maybe his body was thrown into the depths of the sea. We just don't know. Gilprey would never tell us. My Mother was dead, and my sister came back to the camp where we all were. She came alone. She said to us, 'That old man Gilprey has killed my Mother and Father', but nobody took any notice of her. They did not believe her. Everybody was there in the camp and they took no notice of my sister. That old man Gilprey was the boss of that land. The next morning we went out hunting, all of us, me too even though I was young. We found my Mother, we cried; we cried; we cried with intensity and then we buried her there. But Gilprey Walala he had run away in the night, and they searched for him but he had paddled away to another island. They searched for him, but did not find him, in the same way they searched for my Father but we did not find his body. Later, they found Gilprey and we all came east into Borroloola. We had court there. I was small at that time, as was my sister [sic] Hilda. She spoke Yanyuwa then. After the court Gilprey was taken into the west to Fanny Bay. He remained there. We never saw him again. And my sister Hilda, she too went into the west to Port Darwin. Her Mother cried for her as did many others. Hilda is still there at Darwin. She never came back until she was an old lady. She is still there in Darwin, an old lady. After the court, we went down the river to Minngarra on the Batten Creek. There was a big fight there. The fight was because of the death of my Mother and Father. They fought there for a long time. So that is all. I have finished.

In his letter to me John Bradley also told me that,

'The fight mentioned by Ida which took place after you and Gilprey had been taken away is mentioned by old Bill Harney in one of his books. He witnessed the fight at Mingarra. It is on page 165 of his book called North of the 23 Degrees, in the chapter called "Beach Combing Days". It is also mentioned in his book Life Among the Aborigines on page 168 under a heading Totemic Fighting, in the chapter called "The 'Loo and its People". A few of the little details are mixed up, but Gilprey is mentioned as is the Dreaming of Ida's Father, the a-Alanthaburra or chestnut rail, a mangrove bird".

Gilprey's murder of Ida's parents on the Island required us to be called as witnesses. We were all brought in from Vanderlin Island to the police station. Perhaps the policeman Bridgland decided that he had to take everyone to Darwin. He rounded up half-caste kids and took them along too. He must have told my Mum she had to bring me to the police station. We waited there at the station until they rounded up Yellow Minnie's daughter, Sarah, from McArthur Station. She was a white girl. Well, quadroon was what they reckoned. She was very fair and her mother was too. Once Sarah got to the police station, we left for Darwin in a police convoy. Gilprey, the prisoner, plus a lot of my relations were going to be witnesses about the murder on Vanderlin Island.

There was half-caste Hilda, my full blood cousin Ida, and the quadroon Sarah, three up on one horse, all leaving our country. I can't remember now being with my Mother just before I was taken to Darwin. Remembering back over seventy years to something you were never supposed to remember, is hard. I reckon most people remember what happened to them as little kids because their friends and relations remember. The kids can keep checking up, talking it over and over. Nowadays, people have photos to help with memories of long ago. The police recorded our departure this way:

April 8th 1928: Tracker Fred was on Island collecting witnesses in murder case.
April 10th: horse left for McArthur River Station to get quadroon girl Sarah.
Wednesday 11th April: Tracker Fred back from Vanderlin with witnesses Peter—Melba., Ida, Pharoah and Melba on murder charge against Gilbrey (Wil-be-loh). (sic)
On Thursday 13th April the record says that half-caste Hilda Nama was brought to the station by her mother:
Friday 13th: Tracker Harry and quadroon girl Sarah returned from McArthur.
Saturday April 14th at 10.00 am: Gilprey charged with murder of lubra Judy (sic) at Vanderlin Island before Mr Charlie Havey, JP.

Mr Havey had said that the murderer had to go for trial at the next criminal sittings in Darwin. I don't know why Bridgland called my aunt Judy. Her 'whitefella' name was Melba and her tribal name was a-Aralka. More bad ears. Ida and her uncles and aunts were all going to Darwin as witnesses to Gilprey's killings so I don't know why my mother wasn't taken as a witness too. We left Borroloola from outside the dear old pub, Tattersalls Pub, where my mother worked.

On Monday 16 April 1928, the big police convoy with Mr Bridgland in charge left Borroloola. They were taking Gilprey to Darwin to face court for murder and while they were at it, they thought they might as well take me, half-caste Hilda Jarman, and the octoroon Sarah 'to school.' As an old woman, all these years later, I feel really sad for little white-looking Sarah. She spoke only English when she was taken from her home at McArthur River where she'd been treated like she was a little princess. She was put in with a mob of Yanyuwa, all her relations, but we didn't speak any English. Only the police did. She must have felt very frightened and alone.

I remember about four or five horses loaded with supplies, ready for the big trip. It was to be a convoy by horseback. There

34

was no road, only a bush road or track, the one people travelled in the early days to get to places, or for delivery of the mail. It was a very big journey and we travelled through forest country. It wasn't the height of summer but it was still very warm. There were packhorses and maybe a few horses spare so that they could change and rest them. When I picture it, it seems like it was mob of horses. I shared a wonderful, gentle horse.

Old Cliff Lynott, Charlie Havey and old Tim Hogan were probably there, in the dust with the flies, talking, calling out messages to the policeman. My people weren't yelling out to one another, just looking: horses pulling, stamping, shaking heads, harness clicking, dogs barking and squealing when the horses came too near, one big mob of people moving around but staying in the same place. Everyone looked when one saddled horse came up led by the police tracker. He was one of my countrymen, Donegan. Suddenly it was really quiet. Donegan lifted white Sarah, the quadroon, Yellow Minnie's daughter from McArthur, onto the saddle in her hat, smart joddies and riding boots, and she grabbed the reins. Then he lifted me up into the middle and Ida up behind. Ida wrapped her arms around my waist and hung on at the back. This horse was to take us away from our mothers, our culture, all our childhood places forever.

The policeman, tracker and packhorses travelled in front and we were next. Then there was the prisoner, Gilprey. He wasn't too far from the tracker, so they could keep an eye on him. There were also lots of witnesses travelling on foot all the way. They were at the back, following the convoy. I was eight years and three months old and I never saw my poor mother again.

It's funny what you can remember and what you can't. I can't remember whether Mum was there when we left waving me goodbye, and if she was, whether she was crying. Cousin Ida said she cried, along with my other relatives, so she must have been there. If I'd ever spoken to Mum again I'd have asked her how she felt and what she did when I was gone, why she never tried to find me, or if she did. After I was taken lots of other kids went away with the police, west into Darwin. Old people say mothers and aunts followed for days, keeping just behind and watching over their stolen children, some almost as far as Mataranka, all those miles to the railway. Cousin Ida reckoned my mother cried and cried, like all the other mothers. Each year she'd be looking, hoping her little Hilda Jarman would come riding back into Borroloola. Each year her heart was full of dread when her little Hilda didn't come back from Port Darwin in the west.

I had no idea how long the trip from Borroloola was until I saw the police journal record but we stopped to camp, sleep and rest the horses. I remember one place very well: Tanumbrini Station. It wasn't a big camp and there weren't many people living there, just a few white and Aboriginal people. Of course, the policeman went looking for the half-caste kids. That was his job.

Thinking back now, I think this convoy journey wouldn't have been too strange or frightening for me. It would have been just like another walkabout with my relatives. When we started off we were travelling through our country and then we'd have been in country that the older ones would have known about. Whatever I felt later in leaving Borroloola in that convoy I would have been excited about riding a horse for the first time, with little Cousin Ida hanging on to me. All my life I'd gone off with my relatives, sometimes with my mother, travelling for days, hunting food and water, and camping away from the main camp. And just before this we'd all been together on Vanderlin Island. Nearly everyone travelling, even the police tracker, Donegan, was my relative and I'd seen Sarah at the McArthur River Station, when we'd come back from our long walk across the tableland. Ida was my first cousin, and we all knew Sergeant Bridgland.

Perhaps I don't remember Mum crying because it's just too sad to remember. I could never have understood that I was going away forever and wouldn't see any of those people again or that I never would see that place again until I was an old woman with grandchildren.

Usually Aboriginal people aren't too happy with what policemen write down in their records. But when you don't know, or don't remember what happened, it's good to be able to check. In this way I was able to find out what happened seventy years before — Sergeant Bridgland had written it all down in the Borroloola Police journal 1927–31, except that he was writing it as a policeman working under the white law. They were all just doing their jobs — they had no tears and no worries about the old law — Yanyuwa Law. They had no feeling for people who were suffering from being taken away from their country. The old laws were just thrown on the white scrapheap.

When that good old horse took me away from Borroloola on the long journey to Darwin, it changed my life forever. I lost my true inheritance, my ancient language and the culture and loving companionship of my Yanyuwa people. I was not Jarman any more, and never little Yanyuwa a-Marrayimara again. I stopped being an Aboriginal girl and became a half-caste girl. From someone who'd had so much, I was now someone who had nothing with no past and an unknown future, like all those other half-caste kids in Australia who were taken away from their people. From then on, we were expected to shut up, take what the authorities decided was good for us and make our way in life as best we could. And that's what I did, the same as the other children taken and put in homes or fostered. There was no choice.

It's strange the details that policemen put in their journals, but it's good to read now. Bits I remember quite well but most of it's gone from my memory now. In the entry for 15 July 1928, Bridgland starts off:

> Tracker Fred and police horses Blanco, Butcher, Blunt, Blake, Boss, Brock, Concussion, Convoy, Confusion, Verbena and Verdun and foal returned from Darwin.

Then he wrote down all the details. How far we went each day on the outward journey into the west, where we camped and how many meals he gave us on our long trek to Darwin.

16th April — to Billy Days Lagoon — 14 miles HC (that's Sarah and me – half-castes) 6 meals; prisoner 3 meals, witnesses 15 meals; sick abo's 6 meals.

I don't know who the sick people were, but he left them in Darwin when we got there. They didn't go back. Perhaps they had leprosy, TB, or something like that.

17th April — to W. Lagoon — 26 miles.
18th April — To Camp — 23 miles
19th April — to Crooked Creek — 23 miles
20th April — To 8 Mile Spring — 20 miles
21st April — To Tanumbrini Station — 8 miles.

That last one was a pretty short day, but Tanumbrini was the usual stopping place for police convoys. We must have arrived in the morning before dinnertime, one hundred and fourteen miles in six days must have knocked us all up a bit, the little girls on a big horse, with the prisoner and witnesses walking. Ida's and my bare bottoms must have been really sore by then. This was the longest we travelled before getting a decent rest. Sergeant Bridgland and Donegan went over to the Aboriginal camp to see if there were any half-caste kids there.

Nancy Croft told me later when we met up at the Kahlin Home about how her Mum had hidden her in a bag. Maybe it was a big brown sugar bag, a hessian bag, and they made a hole for her to breathe. She was tiny little thing, only about four or five-years-old. The policeman must have known what was in the bag, had probably seen it all before. He asked Nancy's mother to open the bag and there was little Nancy all curled up, so scared she was hardly breathing. But he must have had bit of compassion, that Bridgland, because he left her there. Perhaps he reckoned she was just too little. If not compassion, then commonsense. If he'd taken Nancy he'd have had to look after her all the way to Darwin. So he was different from those missionaries and people who took anyone they saw, pulling tiny ones just weeks, months old, from their mothers' breasts, with their mothers crying and beating themselves and following for miles, wailing and calling, trying to get their babies back. It was terrible, I tell you, just terrible.

A few years later Nancy was put in the Kahlin Compound half-caste Home. This time, though, she was lucky. Not so lucky was poor little quadroon Sarah who was taken away from McArthur River and all her folk, and was here with us, all black strangers, on a horse she didn't know, going to some place she'd never heard about. Only now, when I'm old, do I think about poor little Sarah but she must have been tough little girl because she didn't show any feelings, not on the outside for us to see, anyway. I wonder what her people told her about where she going. I wonder too what my countryman, Donegan, called Tracker Fred by Bridgland, thought about taking us kids away. Maybe he was just a good police boy and didn't think about other black people — he was just doing his job, like a good police boy.

I think somewhere near Tanumbrini there was a jump-up or a cliff and just near that was a little clump of sugar grass which is like small sugar cane. My people love this grass. We suck the stem and get the sugary water out of it. My relatives found some here and gave a handful to the little kids. Maybe they touched the horse's tail with the grass, but he bucked and took off in a great jump. Ida and I hit the hard ground, bottom first. Not Sarah, though, because she could ride. She held the reins and grabbed the saddle. He was a gentle old horse who'd got frightened and thrown us, he hadn't mean to hurt us.

22nd April — To Lagoon Creek — 10 miles
23rd April — To Arnold Run — 24 miles
24th April — To Camp — 24 miles
25th April — To Nutwood Downs — 8 miles

We must have reached Nutwood before dinnertime, moving on eight miles from the night camp. All the stations had their Aboriginal camps down by the creek away from the homestead. The Aboriginal stockmen and their families lived there or near a waterhole in shelters the whitefellas call humpies. That's where we always camped with Donegan to keep an eye on us, to see we didn't go silly and try to get back home or something. Gilprey was in chains.

The Aboriginal women in that camp were all round and chubby and treated us like family. They gave us such a wonderful greeting, those beautiful women at Nutwood. This was the last time I was happy as a little girl, cuddled by round chubby, loving Aboriginal women for the last time.

26th April — To Spring — 23 miles
27th April — to Camp — 20 miles
28th April — To Hodgson Downs — 9 mile
29th April — To Campbell Springs — 26 miles
30th April — To Dagenhardt Lagoon — 26 miles

At Dagenhardt Lagoon my countrymen went swimming and hunting, getting long-necked turtles for us to eat and that must have been the last time I ate food from my country for thirty or forty years. I can't remember anything about the other places we stopped at, just that we ate and slept, tired and sore.

1st May — To Elsey Station — 18 miles
2nd May — To Mataranka Station — 16 miles
3rd May — Camped at Mataranka and knocked all shoes off Police Horses.

We'd travelled more than three hundred miles since leaving Borroloola seventeen days before. At Mataranka we went down to the creek. It was a cold morning and we had a swim and a wash. They gave me Solyptol soap with a lovely strong perfume.

5th May — At 6 p. m. left Mataranka siding for Katherine per Construction train.

I remember as clearly as anything when we left Mataranka in the cattle trucks. We left just on sunset, saying goodbye to the horse that had carried Sarah, Ida and me all the way from Borroloola.

There were no seats in the cattle train and no windows. We were all just herded onto that truck and off we went, sitting on the hard floor, or standing there, hanging on to the high sides. It was frightening for those of us who'd never seen a train before. The police journal entry notes explains that it was a construction train. It wasn't for people, but for carrying what was needed for track building. We kids only knew that the wind in a cyclone could make a big noise. Either a cyclone or thunder. The train engine made frightening new noises for us.

6th May — At 3 am arrived at Katherine. Prisoner locked in cell
7th to 9th May — At Katherine — HCs 18 meals; prisoner in cell 9 meals; Witnesses 45 meals; Sick Abos 18 meals.
10th May — Left Katherine per Train escorting prisoner and arrived Pine Creek 5.30 pm. Handed prisoner and all Abos and Half Castes over to Mounted Constable Turner.

The police journal says we stayed in Katherine for three days. I remember we left Katherine in a proper passenger carriage, with padded seats, staring out the windows. We went whizzing along, passing trees and bushes, in a blur, going past rocky places, over creeks and jump-ups. We had never experienced anything like this. The fastest we could travel back home was walking pace. Not even horses could go this fast. Maybe we thought this was better than walking, or maybe our brains weren't working properly because too many strange things were happening and we were too far away from country.

> **11th May:** left Pine Creek escorting prisoner Gilprey, witness 5, sick abos 2, Half castes 2. Handed prisoner Gilbry (sic) over at 2 mile for Darwin Gaol. Escorted witness,HCs and sick abos to compound, and reported at barracks at 6pm.
>
> **25th June 1928**: on duty at Darwin and attending supreme court re Abo Gilprey charged with murder. Found 'Not Guilty' and discharged.

Gilprey was found not guilty because the courts didn't take evidence from Aboriginal people. Anyway, even if we were sad that Gilprey had killed our relatives, it was a Yanyuwa matter, to be fixed up by our law. It was nothing to do with the white policemen or the judge. Gilprey was a big man for that country, he knew what the Yanyuwa law said. He never went back.

Years later John Bradley told me that if Gilprey hadn't killed my uncle and aunt, I probably wouldn't have been taken from Borroloola. It just happened that way; it was just my bad luck. I'd been in the Kahlin Compound just over five weeks when Gilprey was acquitted and found not guilty. Two days after the trial ended, on 27 June, Sergeant Bridgland left Darwin on the train for Pine Creek with my countrymen, my uncles, aunts, and cousin, police witnesses Melba, Peter, Pharoah, Ida and the other Melba, and someone called 'Abo Leo' they must have picked up somewhere. They took the same track back, stopping at all the same places.

Sarah and I had been taken to Fort Hill railway station. Old Uncle Barney McGinness was the driver of the lorry that picked us up. I think it might have been in an old Bedford or flat-top Ford. We all climbed on and got to the Compound late in the afternoon. Sarah and I were sent off to the half-caste dormitory close to the Kahlin Aboriginal Compound on top of the cliffs in Darwin, Myilly Point, near to where the old Darwin hospital used to be. They put us in the half-caste Home in Schultze Street, what they called the Kahlin half-caste Home. That's how at six at night on 11 May 1928 I stopped being a Yanyuwa child and became a nowhere person. This was also when they gave me my birthdate: 26 January 1920. Australia Day. Motherless, cultureless and stuck in a government institution, not because I'd done anything bad or had been neglected, but because my mother was Aboriginal and my father was not. I ceased to be Aboriginal, but would never be white. I was now something bad, shameful, called a half-caste. Years later they decided that 'coloured' was the new term for all non-whites in the Territory, but we were treated by the whites as if we were bad. Not allowed to fit in one group or another, just kept on our own.

5

Always hungry

The Kahlin Aboriginal Compound was set up to 'contain and control' Aboriginal people living near Darwin. It was an area of six acres, a nice big piece of land, away from the suburbs where the public servants lived, and close to the beach, at what the Larrakia people, the owners of Darwin, called Myilly Point. The whites rounded up all the Larrakia, Wagait and Woolner mob, living as they had for generations along Lameroo Beach and other places round Darwin and put them all in a compound. It might be called protection, but who were they protecting and from what? Anyway, they put a fence around the compound and then they fenced off a separate section further up Schultze Street and called it the half-caste Home for part-Aborigines, little kids like me. Now they had everyone nice and safe, all under control in the Kahlin Aboriginal Compound and in our half-caste children's Home, away from Aboriginal people, even our relations.

Adult Aboriginal people, the ones who worked in town, had to go back to the Compound, the native reserve, to sleep. No-one was allowed to sleep out. After all those generations of living free, Aboriginal people were now like prisoners, prisoners-of-war, locked up in a compound. You had to be behind the compound fence by dark. If you got caught out after curfew time without a permit paper the police would pick you up and you got into big trouble, perhaps having to go to court or gaol for a bit. This curfew was for everyone who wasn't white. No-one was allowed into Darwin, even in the day time, unless they had a permit signed by the Superintendent. Even if you had to go to a doctor, or dentist or something you had to get a permit: 'I hereby give permission for so-and-so to go into town from this time...' And we had to be back at the right time. It was more than a curfew really, it was a ban. The whites were ready to tell us how they were going to let you live in that country. They were really telling us who the boss was now. The same as they decided that we were only good enough to be servants for white people. We could only go to grade four at school so girls learnt to be housemaids and home-helps for the white public servants and the boys learnt to be stockmen, rouseabouts, gardeners or labourers, doing something useful around the place for white people. They gave us half an education and treated us as if we were half human, not white, not black: half an education for half-castes.

I know this now, but back then I was an eight-year-old Yanyuwa child, knowing only Yanyuwa customs, used to the sea and the rivers and eating what our land, rivers, coast, seas and islands gave in season. Now my life was turned right around. Here I was with lots of strange kids crowding round. When I arrived at the Home, all the children were asking questions: What's your name? Where did you come from? Did you get anything to eat?

I don't remember answering any of the questions. I didn't even understand what they were saying. I was frightened to see so many children all so noisy and shouting high-pitched questions that hurt my ears. I was a shy girl, suddenly alone, without relatives in this new world. I only spoke a word or two of English. I was all alone, with skinny little Ida and my aunts and uncles stuck over in the native compound. It was just me, Hilda Jarman, here in the half-caste Home, to be civilised. That's what they said.

Later on we formed special groups of three or four friends. These stong bonds kept us a bit happy. The small groups were special and we stuck with each other through thick and thin. To this day the few of us still around call each other sister and brother. All the children, mine and theirs, respect us and we are Aunty and Uncle to all of them.

We had to make a new family at Kahlin to survive. I don't remember what happened to Sarah after we were put in the Home. She must have been grabbed by another group but we'd never been close. She was so white she didn't stay at the Kahlin Home for long, perhaps a few months. She was taken somewhere else to a different kind of life. Years later I saw her, only now she was Clare. When she was moved from the half-caste Home she was sent to a convent where all the other fair-coloured kids were. The nuns said her name wasn't good enough and told her she was now Clare. That way, when a member of her family asked how Sarah was, the nuns could say, 'We've got no Sarah here.'

In the Home they changed my name from Jarman to Rogers. It was still Hilda, but now Hilda Rogers. That's what I was called until I married in 1940. Where did they get that name Rogers from? Looking back I feel sad for Sarah. She had nobody in the convent, nobody at all. Living on McArthur River Station she'd been treated like a little princess. She must have been a special, favourite kid to have jodhpurs and little riding boots. Now all she had of her old life was speaking English, not even her own name. Mind you, I think it would have been better than the Kahlin Home. At least the nuns weren't starving the kids.

This was 1928 and I settled in to being a half-caste kid living in a Home. I found a special friend, Bridget Johnson, from my country, from Seven Emus Station, east of Borroloola, over towards the Gulf. She was a Garrawa girl and my country-woman–sister. Bridget was like a little sister to me and I had to look after her because she used to carry on like a baby. We'd walk around together, go to bed together and shared everything. We were real mates. You had to have a mate in a place like that. When it was meal time and if you were slow, or crook or something, your mate would get something for you, or share what she'd got. We shared everything — bed, food, secrets.

I remember how frightened we were with the angry Matron and her Army Major husband. We didn't speak our Yanyuwa language not even in whispers under the blanket at night: we were too scared someone might hear us and sing out for Matron and then we'd get flogged for not speaking English. That matron was the worst Gestapo woman I ever met. She and her bully Major husband, the Superintendent of the Kahlin Aboriginal Compound, had just been appointed for four years when I got there, from 1928 to 1932. This seemed like a lifetime. We all lived in fear and dread during those years not even game to think in the Yanyuwa language in case they found out: that's one quick way to have people forget their language and culture — put them in a place where only English is spoken and only white rules are followed and they are forbidden to even remember their life before they became a child in the half-caste Home.

There wasn't much to the Home. Apart from the benches and tables we used for schoolwork, there was no furniture. The bedroom, or dormitory for all the kids was the verandah, closed-in with wire netting and lattice. It was a real tropical verandah with canvas blinds that could be pulled down when it rained. There was no glass in the windows and only one hurricane lamp outside the verandah. That's how we learnt to see in the dark. There weren't beds exactly — maybe a few for the older ones but for most of us bed was a grey blanket on the wooden floor. On very hot nights we put our blanket underneath us and slept on top of it. It was sometimes cold in the dry season and if you were lucky you'd have two blankets. You could sleep on one, with the other on top to keep warm. The big kids would come and roll the little kids while they were asleep and pinch a blanket and the little kids were so tired they'd sleep through.

Every day just before the sun went down, we lined up and were counted, one by one. Six o'clock was the deadline for us to be in the dormitory. They locked us up for the night with two padlocks on the door. One was a big one, like the lock on a jailhouse; the other one was smaller. There were seventy of us and when we were outside we had to stay under the house and as the house was on piers, we played underneath, not around the back where the toilets were, but where we got our meals, underneath.

We were let out at about seven in the morning by the girls going to work. The older girls, maybe twelve or thirteen-years-old, had to go to work as domestics by 7.30 at Myilly Point where the public servants lived. They did the cooking and looked after the little children. Then they came back each night to the dormitory and got locked in with the kids. They were supposed to get six shillings a week but they didn't get their fingers on the money. Most of it was paid into a Trust Account at the Aboriginals Department. It was supposed to be saved for them for the time when they wanted to buy a house or something but years later when they asked for their money they were told there was nothing there. All that hard work for six shillings a week had just vanished. All those hard months of work and nothing to show for it. It must be that white people aren't too good at taking care of those girls' money or something. They were not too worried about accounting for half-castes' wages.

At least the older girls who worked during the day, got away from the Home. They'd go out, find themselves a boyfriend, get pregnant, and come home and have those children. Then they had to go back to work and leave their babies at home. That was before my time; I didn't see it happen in my time but we knew and kept telling the next generation what had happened. The authorities used to pinch the babies while the mothers were away at work and then send them away down south. They'd adopt them out. It was cruel and heartbreaking. Those poor women. That's why when I had my two little children later, Cecilia and Harold, I always took them to work with me. I wasn't going to have them pinched by authorities even if they weren't doing that anymore. You couldn't trust them not to have the bright idea again.

Each morning they'd wake us up and unlock the door with the heavy chain and thick lock as if we were wild animals or something. All the little kids had to go into the yard and clean it by picking up sticks and leaves to make everything look clean and beautiful. Then we'd get into line and wait for the showers even though they didn't work sometimes. I know we had showers but I don't know how we dried ourselves because I can't remember any towels. Then we'd run downstairs for breakfast, sitting in the dirt under the house next to the tables for serving the food.

We never had enough to eat. I don't know why but there was never enough food for us. Whether the Government was mean with the money or whether the Matron and Superintendent pinched it for themselves I don't know. Maybe they didn't count us properly. This is my memory of what we had every day:

> 8.00 am — one ladle of porridge, with goat's milk and a little piece of bread
> 1.00 pm — billabong stew — goat's meat, potatoes and onion
> 5.00 pm — bread, jam or treacle with black tea

Aboriginal women did the cooking in the Compound and then they brought it to the Home in big iron pots, sometimes in kerosene tins. They carried one kerosene tin of tea and one tin of porridge or boiled stew. Kerosene tins were lighter to carry and two women carried them with a stick through the handle. They'd slop the food into our plates or whatever with a big ladle. The bread was a sort of damper and it was quite filling. If you were lucky you got two pieces but if you were late in line you only got one. Sometimes, right at the end, you might get nothing. If kids were punished with no food then the other kids would save a bit of theirs to share so it was important to have a mate to share with.

There were no proper plates or mugs, just some old tin plates. We used tins from tinned food to drink out of and we had hardly any knives and forks. Whatever we'd scrounged to eat we took with us and hid so the other kids couldn't pinch them. We had so little that we hung on like mad to what we did have. Some kids had a bright idea: we could make a hole in a jam tin, put string through it and carry it around all day, or hang it up somewhere under the house. Some kids even used to carry their tins to bed at night but the older kids would wait for them to go to sleep then they'd roll them and pinch the tins for themselves but it wasn't funny because sometimes kids missed out on food.

I don't know how we survived. What they brought to the Home to eat was all there was. If you missed out there wasn't any more for you, or if they put in short rations, bad luck; you just had to be happy with what you got. If you didn't have a tin to drink out of when they handed out tea, you didn't get any. Matron never came to see if we were getting our food. The Aboriginal women from the big Compound came three times a day: breakfast, dinner and supper.

We were always hungry. That's why we used to crawl through the fence to get at the next door neighbour's garbage. We couldn't get over what good stuff they threw out — potato skins, onions and stuff. If you got caught scavenging you'd get a big caning — six cuts: three on one hand and three on the other with a big dry cane and jingey it'd sting, or they'd punish you in other ways by making you stand in the sun with your hands on your head for half an hour, one hour, maybe more. And you'd see Matron peeping out through her window making sure that the child was being punished and standing still in the sun with their hands on their head, not moving. If they moved they had to stand there longer still.

This Matron was the one who kept us the hungriest. She was the worst one there while I was in the Home. I remember her name, but it's not fair to say it. She and her husband have kids and grandchildren now, so it's not right to tell. It was during the Depression and maybe rations were short, but you know what I think? I think she didn't ask for enough to feed us so she could keep the costs down and get in the good books of Dr Cook (the Chief Protector) and the people in Canberra. We were seventy hungry, shaven-headed boys and girls, with no-one to care about us. We were all dressed in old khaki jute romper-suits and had no knickers, just the rough jute. If we tore our clothes we tried to sew them up with small bits of scratchy wire. We tried to cobble them up by twisting the wire in and out of the tear so Matron couldn't see we'd torn our clothes. Torn clothes made her very cross.

Some Kahlin kids had Aboriginal relations living in the native Compound up the road. If they went out to work they sometimes brought a loaf of bread or something so the kids used to hang around the fence, just to get something extra. You weren't supposed to be near the fence and they tried to keep us away from the full-blood Aboriginal people. One day a relation of mine from the Compound, an old countryman named Fat Jack, a police tracker, was going past with his wife. He spotted Bridget and me and he came over and gave me two shillings. Two shillings was a lot of money. We thought it was terrific to have a big shiny two-bob piece.

I gave it to Bridget to look after: 'You look after this now, you look after this.' We thought that shiny, new two-bob piece was the loveliest thing we'd ever seen. We'd never owned anything so lovely. We took it in turns to hold it, turning it this way and that. We weren't going to spend it, no matter how much we wanted food because once we'd spent that coin we wouldn't have anything pretty in our lives. We just nursed it like it was gold.

We should have spent it but it was too special even to buy a loaf of bread from the bakershop delivery man, Jackie Lee. He also sold ice cream and a meat delivery man, Home's Butchers, came past every day. They used to come each morning and deliver bread and meat to the neighbours. When we went to bed we'd throw the two bob under the blanket and go to sleep. It was our special piece of magic. The other kids knew we had the money; there were no secrets in that place. Near school breaking-up time the older girls decided to buy a Christmas present for the old teacher. They were rounding up every little bit of money from anyone who had any. One girl, I know who it was, said, 'Oh I know who's got money, two bob. Hilda and Bridget. They've got two bob.' They rolled us over and took my two bob. When we both got up and picked up our blanket to fold it and there was no two bob, I cried and cried. I blamed Bridget for losing it, poor thing. She said, 'I didn't lose it. It was them big kids came and rolled us, pinched it from under the blanket.' The one who did it, she was a crook. She was a big stool pigeon crawling up to the big girls. I found out later who it was but I blamed poor Bridget.

So we ended up with nothing. No bread, no ice cream, no coin. By keeping my lovely shining magic two-shilling piece, I'd lost everything. Poor little Bridget. I was so nasty to her about it — as if it was her fault. She's dead and gone now.

6

Ringbarking trees

There were wattle and poinciana trees growing in the yard at the Home and we'd scratch them for seeds to chew when we got hungry. We had to scratch the wattle seeds when they fell on the ground, like little chooks or something and we'd chew and suck the dry pods of the poinciana trees. That was when we were really hungry and in pain. Kids from different parts of the Territory would take it in turns to try the food, like trying out bush food. If no-one knew it, then we tested it. If it didn't make you froth at the mouth and fall over it was okay — proper bush food. Across the road from the Home was bush. None of the homes are there today. We'd try to escape, to run over the road and get some bush tucker without being caught by Matron — yams, lizards, berries, anything. We were such hungry, desperate kids. We weren't supposed to go to the bush and most of the time we were shut in the Home so we ringbarked the trees in the yard, stripping the bark and chewing it. That was until the Chief Protector got to hear about it. The neighbours, white people living near the Home, must have seen us out there. They knew we were starving, and they knew we sneaked through the fence to check their rubbish for potato peels, bits of onion, cabbage and stuff. We'd wait until something was put in the bin and then we'd climb over, open the lid and get it out then we'd run like mad in case someone saw us or Matron caught us.

Perhaps the neighbours saw us eating the vines off the fence. Some of those neighbours were good kind people. I remember one family at the back, the Mettams, passed bits of toast to us through the fence. After a lot of complaining from white people, Dr Cook said he'd come around to inspect us all to see if we were getting enough food. Matron told us Dr Cook was coming around and that when he asked if we were getting enough to eat we had to say yes, if not we'd get a big flogging when he left. We were so scared we didn't say anything. Only, 'Yes, we get enough.' We were too frightened to tell the truth. no-one in power ever got to hear about how we were hungry all the time. It's amazing that Dr Cook only asked the woman he put in charge if she was starving us. What else would she say? Did we look like we were well-fed? Or did we look like we were living on treebark and vines, anything we could get our hands on.

Maybe Matron blamed the Aboriginal women in the Compound. She might have said they weren't reliable and weren't giving the kids enough to eat and that's exactly why we have to take them away from their Aboriginal mothers and put them in a half-caste Home. They shaved our heads so that they could be sure we did not have nits. They cleaned our jute romper-suits ready for inspection day. Because we had shaved heads and jute romper suits it was not possible to tell if we were boys or girls.

Dr Cook felt good that these white officials were saving us kids from all the half-caste things white society is so frightened of. He wrote to Canberra and told them how good they must all feel, saving half-caste kids from nits and starvation and parental neglect. The churches helped in running the homes, so we hardly cost the white taxpayer anything. Maybe that was the best of all: everyone could feel good, specially if it wasn't costing any money and we were eating treebark and rubbish. It was very cheap to feed the Kahlin Compound kids. It was easier to shave heads than to wash and brush hair.

But Bridget had wonderful long hair, a lovely long thick mop of ringlets. Every morning she'd come running around to get her hair done, ready for school. I'd say, 'Go and find a fork.' A fork was the only thing we had for a comb. There were no combs, no brushes, no mirrors and we'd try to pull it through her hair to make it look good for school. I don't know if she had long hair all the time, or if I remember her long hair because trying to comb it with a fork it was so hard and so silly. The things you remember from those years are bits and pieces because they were hard times and you survive by not remembering the bad bits. Except some things stand out in your mind and were very real and scary, like Matron's husband, that big bully Major, and the swishing noise the cane made as Matron whipped your hands and the sharp 'clack' it made as it hit your palms or caught us across the calves of your legs. We would be sore for days. I remember that alright. There was one nasty memory that stayed. One girl used bad language, a four-letter word or something and someone ran and told Matron. I don't know why we always told on one another. Maybe we hoped Matron would think we were good and would not be so hard on us if we told her what was happening. But it happened all the time. The poor girl tried to run away but they caught her and brought her back. She was taken into Matron's front garden where we could all see. That big Army Major Superintendent whipped her with a 'cat-thing', three-tails, you know, with the leather strips. They whipped her bare back until it bled. Then Matron wrote something on a big piece of cardboard and tied it on her back and the poor girl had to parade around the yard, letting everybody know what would happen if you swore. This girl was about eleven at the time, poor thing. We got caned for petty things. It seemed like Matron just liked to put the boot in, whenever she could just to scare the kids.

When Matron reckoned someone was really bad she got her husband to flog us, sometimes with a dry cane stick and sometimes with a green-stick cane, five on this hand, five on that, or on our legs. When we were caned or whipped it was always in front of everyone so everyone would know what would happen if we were naughty. It shamed us too. Matron and her husband liked to punish little kids with an audience as if it gave them more power or something.

Looking back on it now, although I can't say I had good times there, I don't remember that we had that many really unhappy times either. Not most of the time. After a while we just accepted our life and lived day after day. We just got used to the way things were. We had our mates and we were like brothers and sisters, one big family of seventy little kids. We enjoyed each other's company and what mattered most to us was that we cared for one another. We used to get into fights, like kids in all families but soon we'd get over it and all live together, playing games and all that sort of thing. As I've said, when I first went there the Matron was a very, very hard woman and after the sort of life I'd lived round Borroloola with my loving Yanyuwa people, the floggings, hearing and speaking only English instead of language, sleeping in a house, remembering all the rules about things — all of this had a bad effect on me. I think that's why I was a meek, scared thing for so many years. Maybe that's why I don't remember more about my time in the Home. I didn't want to remember, or something. I was scared of white people and speaking to strangers. It was years before I got used to talking to strangers and it took me many more years than that to stand up for myself, and look people in the eye.

You know, in the bad old days there were kids who were so mad to get away they'd put the juice from milk trees in their eyes so they had to go outside to a doctor. One time a girl put a small pebble in her ear. It was a silly thing really, but they had to take her to a doctor and so she went into the outside world. We were desperate just to get away from that Home. The outside world seemed like paradise to us. We didn't really know what it was like but we imagined living there. All our problems would be gone once we were outside.

One really good time for us was when we got whooping cough. Dr Cook only really came to the Home when there was an outbreak of serious sickness and this was probably in late 1931. He decided that we should be taken away and isolated on an island across the harbour so the townspeople wouldn't catch whooping cough from us. My uncle from Borroloola, old George Campbell, was in charge of us while we were there. He took us by launch, trip after trip, across the channel to the old quarantine station. Being over at Channel Island was a happy time. We stayed there for six or eight weeks. It was heaven to be running wild, sixty or seventy kids running wild, no school, just going mad, hunting and fishing, getting food off the land again, sugar-bag from the trees or an ant bed, swimming, digging for roots and things, catching goanna. The whooping cough time was really a good time for us half-caste home kids. We lived in the old buildings there. Some years later they turned the island into a leprosarium.

After that measles was a big let down. I got measles but we just stayed in the Home. There was no Channel Island adventure this time. No roaming and fishing and swimming like real little black bush kids. When I got measles I remember my nose running and that my eyes were watering and sore and I stayed inside away from the light. Overall we were surprisingly healthy kids. I don't know why, maybe because we lived so tough.

Not long after I came to the Home, my cousin Babe Damaso heard I'd been brought down. He was on one of the nightcart trucks that picked up the pans from the toilets. In the old days every house had a pan lavatory and these men used to work in teams taking the pans away and putting in new, empty ones. When he heard I was in the Home he got somebody to get me. I must have been about nine or ten years old. A girl came running calling out, 'Hilda, come here. I'll show you something. Someone wants to have a look at you.' When I saw it was a man, I was so shy I ran away thinking I didn't know him. He called out to me and I saw it was my cousin Babe and he just wanted to see me. He must have gone home and told his father dear old Pop Damaso, that I was down there in the half-caste Home. So Pop came round to visit me. I remember him coming to the fence. The kids said, 'Hey, that man wants to see you, Hilda,' and they took me to the fence to see this short Filipino man. I was scared because I wasn't supposed to go near the fence, but somehow the kids got me to go to see this old little man and talk to him. I was scared of getting into trouble and being punished but he was talking away in the Borroloola lingo that I could now not understand. I know it wasn't all that long after I'd gone into the Home but I didn't understand what he was saying. Maybe it had been too long and I was too scared to be able to understand. In the Home we were punished if we didn't speak English and we lived with that dread inside of us, that fear.

I was in the Home with all the other half-caste kids to learn to be civilised and to be educated. We went to school in the Home and my favourite teacher was a very kind lady. I think she felt sorry for us and our lot. She lived in a house just down from the Home and she'd come after breakfast and teach us from half-past eight until half-past three. We called her old Mother Carruth. She was a dear old thing. She used to let some of the little children touch her. We never touched anyone, really, and no-one ever touched us, except to belt us, or give us a shaking. I think I was one of her pets as she always seemed so kind to me. If you did a little bit of work, more than she'd asked, she'd put a lolly under your slate. That's what we used to do our school work on, slates with a thin slate pencil. It used to squeak if you held it a certain way when you were writing.

First we started learning our ABCs then we began to write a few words. I was slowly learning to speak English like most of the other kids. Some of them, those who'd been there longer, were quite good at it. We started out with words like 'cat' and 'mat'.

Then, when we got into grade one, we were given sentences to write. It was all very slow I suppose, but then no-one expected us to be clever or to be good at school. Later in grade one we began things like arithmetic and 'mental'. I was good at both of those. We did geography but I didn't like that so I wasn't any good at it, or history. Another thing I found hard was drawing. My friend who used to sit next to me in those days, was no good at arithmetic but very good at drawing so we used to help each other out. Cheating didn't fool old Mrs Carruth. She knew what we were doing but she used to make a joke of it. She'd tell us off but that's as far as she went. When I think what the other people were like who had charge of us I realise what a wonderful, gentle person she was. Even when people were naughty she hardly caned them. I never got the cane.

When she went on holidays there was a Mrs King and a Miss Haines, but my favourite was Mrs Carruth. I knew she was fond of me because she was always watching me, you know, and when I was about twelve or thirteen she told me that she and her husband wanted to foster me because they had no children and they wanted to have someone to leave their stuff to, instead of the government taking it. I didn't know anything about that but I was rather shy and a bit frightened. Anyway, she kept on asking me, 'Would you like to come or not?' So I said, 'Yes.' She must have told Matron or got in touch with the Chief Protector and said that she and her husband wanted to adopt me. Dr Cook made a time to come and see me and that's where Matron stepped in.

She got me in her room and said 'Hilda, Dr Cook is coming to see if you want to go to with Mrs Carruth. Now, I want you to say "No" to Dr Cook because Mrs Carruth only wants you for her slave. I think she wants you to be there for her husband. I only want what's best for you.' I didn't know what to think. There was no-one I could talk to so when the Chief Protector Dr Cook asked me if I wanted to go to live with the Carruths I was so frightened Matron would belt me I said 'No'. I did what I'd been told to and I must have hurt dear old Mrs Carruth but I was too frightened of Matron to say yes. She just didn't want anyone to have an opportunity. When I think about it now, Mr and Mrs Carruth must have been hurt and disappointed. They wouldn't know that Matron had told me to say 'No' to Dr Cook or I'd get the cane. They must have felt funny that I didn't want to take the big chance they gave me, and I was too shy to tell Mrs Carruth what had happened. We were so used to doing what we were told that we just went along and accepted decisions whether they were good or bad.

We tried to have fun in the Home and when we weren't in school or cleaning the yard or sleeping, we played games — chasey, rounders and something called dog-and-the-bone, games like that. We didn't have much to do when we weren't in school, cleaning or sleeping. Some of the girls, took up dress making when they got a bit older and learnt to make dresses or romper suits. Somebody must have heard what a tough life we had and thought they could give us a happy outing. This was the man who ran the Don Pictures — the open-air pictures, so we used to go to the pictures, usually on Wednesdays, which was the night they showed cowboy movies. We loved this. We had to sit right down the front on wooden seats with the full-blood people from the Compound. Canvas chairs were just for the top people — whites only. These were racist times and whites were whites and blacks were blacks, but we loved those cowboy films — Hopalong Cassidy, Roy Rogers and all those old stars; Gene Autry and Randolph Scott too. We didn't go every Wednesday but we did go a few times.

Sometimes, if we were very lucky, Matron told the cook or one of the older girls to take us down to Mindil Beach on a Saturday, not every Saturday though. Sometimes we went to Cullen Beach. We loved it there because there'd been a Chinese garden there at one time so we could still find fruit things to eat, including guavas, mangoes and coconuts. There were lots of coconut trees and we used to climb them and pick the nuts and have a good feed. They were tall trees and I was good at climbing. I was like a little monkey — up there so fast, grabbing and twisting the nut, then letting it go. It was a lovely beach and even though we couldn't fish because we didn't have fishing lines, we collected periwinkles and other shellfish. We also swam — we used to swim for as long as we could. It was good when we went to Mindil or Cullen, but this happened only once in a while when Matron was in a good mood.

It was that special to get away from the Home. I remember that we used to go out on Empire Day, Queen Victoria's birthday, the twenty-fourth of May. We thought she was alive. That was a big picnic day at Mindil Beach when the whole town celebrated the old Queen's birthday and we looked forward to it. We had lollies — lots of lollies.

It must have been about 1932 when I was twelve that the bad Matron and her husband finally left and things changed. We could grow our hair again and we began to think we really were human children after all.

Things started getting better. It was just those early years, from 1928 to 1932, that life was so bad for me. In that time we all felt sad most of the time, being taken away from our people and our country, and then we had that feeling of dread. We never knew when the Matron was going to get cranky and punish us or have her husband flog us. I don't know how naughty we were really, and it was a big job with seventy children, but the people who came in after them kept control and there was hardly any caning and no flogging with a three-tail whip. We had more trips away from the Home too. Life was starting to get better.

7

Feeling human

What the Government was doing was trying to find the right people, like a husband-and-wife team, to run the Aboriginal Compound. The husband was to be the Superintendent and his wife the Matron. They were offering short-term contracts: four years, I think, or three; but some stayed only twelve months. We had a number of people come through to manage us. One particular policeman was a giant of a man with big boots. He was an arrogant fellow and used to come into the dormitory in the night if he thought we were still talking. He'd open the door and everybody would hold their breath and make out they were sleeping. Walking in, he'd say 'Who's been talking, then?' Everybody kept really quiet, as if we were dead. 'I know you're not asleep,' he'd say and boot you in the leg or the backside or something. And you'd just lie there, really scared, making out you're asleep. He wasn't a nice man and it was good for us that he was only there for twelve months. It's funny how men with big boots like kicking skinny little half-caste kids.

The people who replaced this Superintendent were the Heathcocks and they made such a difference to our lives. Mounted Constable Ted Heathcock and his wife, Sister Ruth, a nursing sister took over and stayed for about two years. This was when I was about twelve. After she'd been there for a while Sister Ruth started making frocks for the girls. As we were getting a little grown up she decided we should be wearing frocks, so she started making them from her old uniforms. Up until then we'd never worn anything but clothes made from thick dungaree or khaki material. My first frock was pleated and I felt really smart in it. I liked how I looked. When she gave it to me, it was the first time I felt like a human being. I felt like I was being recognised as a young woman for the first time. Sister Ruth showed us compassion, caring and real love. It was wonderful after what we'd felt while the awful ones were there. Whites being kind and loving was a new experience for us. We now felt like we were living in a family environment rather than being treated like a mob of cattle in a yard.

The Heathcocks used to take us to the beach. There's a photo of us down at Mindil or Cullen Beach. And I've got one of Ruth and Ted with some of us in front of the Superintendent's place. Ted always wore a pith helmet. They were good for keeping the sun away and cooled the head. Ted was a big, handsome man and Ruth was a tall, good-looking woman with a really sweet face that made you think you could trust her as soon as you saw her. They both had it and you just knew they loved each other. They smiled a lot and maybe that made us feel easier about being looked after by strangers. There wasn't so much anger around the place, and they acted as if they liked us. This felt more like living in a real family.

When we left home we became aware of the limitations of our training and schooling. When we were twelve or thirteen our training consisted of being designated a small area of the dormitory which we were expected to scrub. When we were seven, eight or nine, we were designated a small area of the school-yard which we had to keep clear of leaves or grass. We'd never had any proper training and only bits and pieces of school work — spelling, writing and a bit of reading. We did history and geography too. I only went as far as Grade 3. We weren't learning anything about how to live or to care for ourselves or our kids or things like that. And we had no social skills. All we knew was to live and to do what we were told. We'd had no example of how to live in a real family, and we'd had no proper furniture either. In the day time we'd eat our meals off tin plates and drink from tin cans while sitting in the dirt. In the night time we would lie together, huddling under the blankets we had as one to keep warm. Once we reached the age of fourteen we could no longer stay at the Home and were sent into the world. Everything was new, especially meeting people. I'd been taken from the bush, running around eating bush tucker and locked up for six years in a government institution and then sent out to work. Just like that. I didn't know how to live outside the Home.

When I left the Home in 1934, the year I turned fourteen, I went to work. I was disappointed I could not go on at school, however it was government policy in those days that I could not. Dr Cook was the Chief Protector then and administered the rule that half-caste girls would get taught nursing so that they could look after Aboriginal people. He gave us the choice of doing domestic work for public servants or training to do a bit of nursing for Aboriginal people. My writing was always neat and I was quite good at English and arithmetic, so he said, 'Hilda, you're all right, good enough to start nursing.' Just before school was to begin again, Dr Cook directed me to leave the Home and start a new life training to be a nurse. He thought some of the girls and I could take over part of the job of the Kahlin Home's Matron, going down to treat some Aboriginal women with gonorrhoea. There was an older native woman at the Aboriginal Compound who helped do the job too.

I remember leaving the Home. You just went out to face a new life, but you didn't know the world outside and we'd never mixed with people from the outside. I suppose I went with Daisy Cusack and Polly Kelly who were nurses. We used to have a green uniform with a white collar and cap which was nice.

We left the Kahlin half-caste Home and stayed at the old hospital in Packard Street, over towards Larrakia. I was very excited about training to be a nurse. I'd always liked playing nurse in the Home and now I was going to learn to be a real one. And that's when I caught up with my beautiful cousin Mary Damaso again. It was beginning to be a better time for me. We would start walking from the nurses' accommodation at the hospital quarters at 7.30 am, do our work, then walk back to the quarters after we'd finished.

After I'd been nursing at the Hospital for a while, my Kahlin sister Bridget arrived there too as a nursing aide. I remember showing her around, but after a while she left nursing and went as a domestic for Mr and Mrs Wing.

In those days you still had to follow the permission law; you had to ask to go into town, so we didn't have our own freedom. It didn't matter whether we were working or not. We didn't have to carry a certificate, we just had to have verbal permission. The coloured people who lived in the town, had to carry a permit. Although we were now out working, living away from the Home, because we were wards of the State we still had the Chief Protector to keep an eye on what we were doing, where we were going, who we were seeing. We still had to be under the escort of older girls who were more or less given the responsibility of being our guardians. I liked going out to the pictures.

We were allowed out once a week. There was an older Aboriginal woman nursing there then and as the authorities thought she could handle the responsibility, we would be escorted to the pictures once a week. This was in Mrs Roy Edwards' time. She was a nice woman and the Matron of Darwin Hospital. I was only young then, and had to have somebody keep an eye on me. At the pictures, there were boys, a mob of town boys, hanging around and looking at us, and we'd look back. We didn't try to meet them or anything. We didn't encourage them, but they just kept hanging around, anyway. And they'd sit right behind us at the pictures, putting their feet up and pushing us in the back with their feet and their knees. You know how boys are. We couldn't do anything and I was a bit frightened. I'd never known anything like this before and was a bit scared of the noisy boys who also went to the pictures.

I met Billy Muir for the first time at the pictures and straight off I thought he was the most handsome boy. I fell in love with him and I've never stopped loving him. I didn't stop to think about whether being in love with him was a good idea or not.

Billy was the foster son of Sarah and Jim Scully. Old Jim Scully was what they used to call a, Kanaka'. He had been taken as a slave from one of the islands, captured to work as a sugar cane-cutter. But he travelled from Queensland to the Northern Territory where he'd met Sarah. Sarah was from Hodgson Downs, way over toward Borroloola. She was an Aboriginal woman and a very good horsewoman when she was younger. Like Jim, capable, clever, but also tough, hard and fierce. Jim was a fencing contractor and used to fence on Willeroo Station, 70 miles southwest of Katherine, when old man Roney was the manager there. Bob Muir, Billy Muir's father was working in the office on Willeroo and old Nellie Narmawood, a Wardaman woman from Manbullo Station, about eight miles out of Katherine, had a son with old Bob Muir, and that was Billy. He was born on Willeroo Station; a bush birth on his mother's country, like me. No-one was there to register him but Bob Muir gave him his name anyway. Billy was born close to when Jim and Sarah Scully's son, William, was born, so they reckoned his date of birth was near enough for both of them. There was always a strong bond between these two boys.

Old Bob Muir had a brother, Ernest Clare Muir, who came to the Territory because the New South Wales police were looking for him for cattle duffing. So, like lots of other men who came to the Territory, he changed his name and went by the name Jim Campbell. He used to work over near Borroloola and around Katherine. The spring near Borroloola was called Campbell

Springs after him. He was legendary. He was killed by an Aboriginal man who speared him. He was buried at Kings River.

Jim Scully got a contract with Vesteys to fence along Victoria River and Willeroo. After this contract was finished the family came to Darwin so the children could get an education. Billy's mother asked Sarah and Jim to take Billy so that he wouldn't be taken by the police to a Native Institution. Bob Muir, Billy's real father, was a Scotsman and did not stay with Nellie or Billy. Billy worked like a man when he was only a little kid — cutting ironwood for posts, carrying wood, straining the wire tight and doing other jobs with old Jim and the boys.

I was in love with Billy. I didn't want to marry a white bloke — maybe because my white father hadn't claimed me.

The law said that Billy needed permission to court me because I was a Ward of the State. There was never any 'boy meets girl' stuff for State Wards like me. Dr Cook, the Chief Protector, played the role of father to us. He liked to arrange marriages for girls from the Home, usually to white men. Everyone knew that Dr Cook arranged marriages for white men and they then got good positions working as domestics for public servants. Dr Cook would choose special half-caste girls to line up. Like a police line-up, the men looked at them, and then chose the one they liked. Then the half-caste girl and the white man would get married with Dr Cook's blessing and the man would get a good job. It wasn't romantic, but it was a good way of escaping the Compound. Sometimes he even found a nice house for the white men as an extra pay-off for marrying a half-caste ward from the Home. Really this was a way of breeding out the colour in us. That was the official policy in those days.

Dr Cook said that it was alright for Billy Muir, as an exempt half-caste boy, to court me, a half-caste Ward of the State. It was just as well. Because that same week I got on the train for Katherine, and ignorant of such things, I noticed I didn't get my February period. While I stayed in Katherine I stayed with other Aboriginal nursing aides. We lived in little huts away from the main hospital building in Katherine.

The real character around the place was Dr Fenton. He was the doctor-in-residence and the first flying doctor. The airport wasn't far from the hospital and any time he was called out, he just went. If there were any accidents out in the bush, he'd just hop in his plane and go. He used to fly so low that one time he nearly hit the top of the hospital roof. He used to act the goat and everyone loved him, even the official who knew he was a dare-devil who flew without a licence.

When he was called out because someone was injured, he hopped in the plane and told the station manager to clear a space for him to land his Tiger Moth. He didn't ever worry if it was dangerous. He was a very brave man. Once he landed in the main street and everyone crowded round, especially the kids. Everyone laughed when he got out of the cockpit, jumped to the ground, popped in to Kirby's pub, had a beer, and then took off again. Lots of people would have died in the bush, without him. They've got his plane in the Katherine Museum now. During the War they named Fenton Airstrip after him.

The Sister at the hospital decided she'd teach me how to prepare the landing lights for night flying. There was no electricity there, so for the plane to land at night you lit flares. A young Aboriginal boy kept the drums filled with fuel so I had to prepare them, making sure they were full. Then we could light them when the doctor was coming in to land in the dark. We had a kind of gun for flares: amber was get ready, blue was okay and red was for danger; don't land.

One day Dr Fenton asked me 'Hilda. Do you want to come in the plane with me?' So I went. Everyone wanted to go up in that plane, but he'd asked me and I loved it. It was amazing looking at the world from up there with the river winding through, and the roads. I only went up once but I wish I'd gone again.

So there I was in Katherine, sixteen-years-old and training for nursing. When I was off duty, I'd wear trouser things, jodhpurs. Daisy had warned me before I went to Katherine that to get to town from the hospital was a two-mile trip. She said to send one of the boys, one of the patients, over the river to ask Bert Nixon for a horse. The boy would cross the river when the water was low and old Bert would saddle up a horse and send it across. Once a week I'd go into town on horseback. During that time my pregnancy started to show, especially since I had to wear jodhpurs when I rode to town.

I was heart broken when they sent me to Katherine because I was in love with Billy. I knew that I must have been pregnant once I felt a baby moving inside me, but I wasn't sure because I'd never been told that menstruation stopping was a sign of pregnancy, or other important 'facts of life'. When it was pointed out to me by Sister Kirk that I was pregnant, I was sent back to Darwin to a Native Full-blood Compound where I was to live in the cottage for unmarried mothers.

By August I was back in Darwin, in the Compound, waiting for my baby. Xavier Herbert was now the Superintendent of the Aboriginal Compound and he and his wife were nice people. She was a very quiet woman. I don't know where she came from. Perhaps she was Maltese. Mr Herbert didn't believe in us begging for anything. When we had to ask to go anywhere, he'd say, 'Cut it out, saying "please". Just come straight out and say, "Can I go in to town?" Not this "please" all the time.' He thought it was terrible that grown women had to ask permission, sort of plead, to do something ordinary like shopping, going to the Trust Fund at the welfare or the pictures.

He was a hard, tough-looking man, but he wasn't cruel, he just had hard mannerisms. I was there in the Compound under Xavier Herbert when Cecilia was born, on 23 September 1936. Billy Muir liked the name Cecilia because he thought it sounded pretty. I took twelve months off after Cecilia was born and then I got a job. By this time, Dr Cook had opened up a new clinic for venereal disease, for VD patients, out at the old quarantine station on East Arm. He opened the clinic and rounded up all the coloured women in town to be checked. The soldiers would say who they'd been with: this one, that one, and so the women had to be checked, and if they had VD they were put on the island. While I had Cecilia as a baby I'd go by the native compound truck out to East Arm Island every day and do the treatments with Dr Cook. That was my new job. Once the women were cleared of venereal disease they closed the clinic.

I took my little girl with me to work, each day. It wasn't good, but I was so scared they'd come and take my baby while I was at work, the way they had in earlier times. It was a terrible tragedy for those young mothers to come home from work and find their baby had just vanished. I don't know if they sent the ones that looked white away down south. It wasn't happening when I was there, but I didn't take any chances. It must have been heart-breaking for those poor mothers and I knew just how they felt. Even if the poor mother asked, the authorities would never tell where the baby was. By then they'd probably changed the name and the mother could never find her little one. And the little ones would never find out who they were and where their real country was. Even when they were grown up. Lots of people were like that. So I always took Cecilia with me to work; to make sure no-one grabbed her and adopted her away.

The thing I loved best about having babies was when I hugged them, and cuddled them and gave them kisses. I loved that bit.

Baby Cecilia and I lived there until the Compound closed. We shared a dormitory with other women. Our children slept with us in our beds. We were still locked up at night. Gradually more and more houses were built around Myilli Point. Now that Billy and I had a child, he used to come around and take me out sometimes. It sounds dreadful now, but we used to call Sarah Scully 'Ma Scully' and sometimes we would stay at her place. We gradually got to know each other.

Harold, our second child, was born on 25 April, Anzac Day, in 1939. This was about the time I first met up with my brother Harry Gore. He'd come back from the Kimberley, where he'd been working as a drover after he left the Catholic Mission on

Bathurst Island, at fourteen years of age. He used to drove the cattle route across from Queensland to the Kimberley. It was a dangerous route; the old Murranji Track. My baby Harold was about a month old when my brother Harry came to visit me. He was a very good brother, concerned for my welfare and the welfare of his niece and nephew. Baby Harold was named for him and his uncle always brought goodies when he visited on paydays — fruit and luxuries.

Billy and I were still not married then. Billy was living with the Scully family in Daly Street, Darwin. One of the Scully boys had bought a block of land up where the golf links are today. The Scullys built a small tin-and-wood cottage and Bill lived with them there. In those days, people didn't have much in the way of houses but it was strongly built, and cool, because everything was open with windows all around. It was up on a rise, looking down to the flat below.

Billy always had a job but as the government took most of his pay and put it in a trust fund, there wasn't much money to go round.

Billy's reaction to Harry was interesting. He ignored the fact that Harry didn't like him and just treated him, like a loving brother-in-law. In the end, William Scully, his foster-brother, told Billy, 'You've got two kids now. You must marry Hilda. If not, don't call me brother again.' Sarah and Jim Scully had come around by this time and they wanted us to get married, too. I knew they liked me, although I think Sarah thought I was quiet.

After a while Billy decided we should get married and we had our big day in the Darwin Registry Office on 30 July 1940. Mr J.W. Nicholls who'd lived near to Kahlin when I was a child, was the celebrant.

After we were married I moved out of the Bagot Compound into the Scully house in Daly Street. There was no water laid on so we had to go to a well which was where the golf links are today. The men would carry two 44-gallon drums on a stick across their shoulders. They had to walk up and down a steep hill which was hard work. With all of us there, and our two children, there was a lot of noise so after a while Billy Muir said we were too cramped and he asked my cousin Babe Damaso if we could get a place of our own out at Police Paddock, where all the coloured people lived. Police Paddock was where Stuart Park is now. Babe gave us a room and we stayed there for a while until we found a house. People at Police Paddock had small huts but there was nothing nearby; just rainwater tanks and kerosene hurricane lamps. This was a sort of half-way camp for coloured people, coming in to Darwin but it wasn't like the old Compound with a Superintendent and strict rules.

Later, Billy met up with Johnny Baird, now married to Bridget Johnson, my little mate from the Kahlin days. They had a house on a good block over at Fanny Bay. There was still open land there, with a bit of scrubby bush. There were no houses, just the Ross Smith Airstrip and the old Fanny Bay jail.

Billy's idea was to move from Cousin Babe's place out to the Baird's block at Fanny Bay and live there in a shed. That's when Bridget and I used to go hunting for bush tucker in the scrub near their house. They had a good dog, a big black thing called Nigger. He was a good hunting dog, so we'd hunt with him and grab whatever he pulled up. Goanna, bandicoot: all good for the pot and it helped with the housekeeping. We didn't wander far from their place; we just followed Nigger to see what he'd found. We went around the edge of the wilder bits of scrub, outside their boundary, but we never trespassed. That was us, hunting for bush tucker in Fanny Bay.

Billy was with the Public Works for a while, but he transferred to Native Affairs in 1941. Native Affairs had started building houses for Aboriginal people in about 1939. They built three or four welfare houses out at Larrakia, one in Schultze Street and another one not far from Schultze Street. We always reckoned they must have used the money from the Aboriginal Trust Fund. We reckoned we sort of paid for those houses ourselves and that the government used the interest from the money paid into that

Trust Fund from our wages. We got a house in Schultze Street, not far from where the Home was and down that side of the street. We stayed there until January 1942, when the rest of the women and children were evacuated to Brisbane because of the war in the Pacific. By this time, Bill and I had had our third child and second son, William Muir.

8

The Big Smoke

Before the War started, Bill had joined the Militia, what they called the Civilian Mobile Forces. A lot of local Aboriginal men joined during 1938 and 1939 and Bill was in the Militia from the early days. When the Army came to Darwin in 1939 he was doing defence work, guarding the oil tanks on McMinn Street. In 1942, when the Japanese were coming, Bill and some of the others were called up into the AIF. From December 1941 on, the authorities were thinking about evacuating families, the women and children, from Darwin. Most people were going by boat to Brisbane and other safer places. Bill had a friend, old Vin White in Native Affairs who had once been the Superintendent of the Aboriginal Compound but was now the Director of Native Affairs in the Territory. After the War began he was the ARP warden for Schultze Street and Bill was made a warden, too. So, when my three children and I needed to be evacuated to Brisbane, Vin found room for us on a DC6, which was much quicker than going by sea.

In January 1942 I left Darwin, Billy and our first little home. Cecilia, Harold and baby Bill, then about three months old, and I flew to my new life in Brisbane. We travelled on the plane with Mrs Molly Anderson and her daughters — Rita and Hannah. We landed at Archerfield Aerodrome and Sarah Scully took us to the Salvation Army Hostel. Sarah was expecting her girls Mona, Francis and Gladys and Gladys's two children who were coming by steamer. At the hostel was Mrs Anderson with her two girls, and Mary Morris, who had one daughter. And then there would be Sarah and her two older daughters, and her little ones, Joseph and Francesca and her two grand children, and me and my three children. That was too many people for the hostel so Sarah decided to find a house to fit us all in. We all wanted to stick together because we were strangers there. Sarah Scully was like a fairy godmother, trying to make sure we all stuck together. She found a big house at a place called Rainworth so we all moved in. It must have been six adults and eleven children. Bill was happy we'd gone to Brisbane because Sarah Scully was already there and he knew she'd look after us. Sarah had arrived before us because she had had to take her youngest son, Michael, to Brisbane for medical treatment.

One day Sarah decided to show us the main city area. You could just walk across the bridge, Victoria Bridge, down to Queen Street. The kids' eyes were all eyes popping: tall buildings and food stores here, there and everywhere. Harold said, 'Mum, this is good place, eh? We're not going back to Darwin.' I'll never forget that. My eyes were popping, too. Darwin was just a bush town then. There was nothing much there really; no big buildings like Brisbane. To come down and see such a huge place with high-rise buildings and with window shopping and the market with fruit stalls outside, such beautiful fruits. And it was, I don't know, sort of frightening. We were with Sarah and she was walking along with all the confidence in the world but I was just too frightened. She was a strong lady, Sarah. There was her baby, Michael, in hospital, to have a growth removed from his face, a swollen infection from his mouth nearly up to his eye. Then she had the rest of her men stuck in Darwin with the bombing, yet she still looked after all of us and never showed she was worried. They removed the growth from Michael's face and the swelling gradually went down, but every day Sarah went and sat with her little man. He was a long time in hospital and when he was ready for discharge they send him down to the Children's Convalescent Home at Redcliffe. Today he's a handsome man and you'd never know he'd had that awful growth on his face as a little boy.

Sarah found a big house and garden for us in Rainworth and she took out a lease on it. It made us all feel safer and happier to be together with Godmother Sarah to look after us, but after about a month the neighbours began complaining about too many of us being in the one house. They were saying that it was unhygienic. The police said that we couldn't live together and they rang places where we could move to so that it was more hygienic. That's when the authorities had to find houses for us evacuees. Mona and Gladys and my family were sent down to the CWA Holiday Hostel, about nineteen or twenty miles out of Brisbane, near Wynnum and Manly. This was a holiday resort place where people came from the country for a holiday by the seaside. During the War the hostel had to house evacuees. They must have found a house for Mrs Anderson, as she and Mary Morris and their kids went together. Sarah and her younger children, Francis and Joseph, stayed in the big house.

The new hostel was way up on the hill, so we used to walk round the hill where the little shop was, to get things. On my way to the shop one day I ran into Mrs Roney, a lovely Territorian lady, and her daughter Monica. Mr Roney had been the Manager on Willeroo Station when Jim Scully had the fencing contract there. I was still a bit shy but it was lovely to see another family from Darwin.

The hostel was near the sea and it was a lovely place, really, where we all had a room each. I don't know how long we were there, it must have been a couple of weeks, when Sarah rang the hostel, to see how her girls were going. In the meantime, she looked for another house so she could have her family together again not so much me, but her daughters. The next minute the two sisters-in-law started packing up. When I asked them why they were leaving they told me their Mum had got a house for them. 'We're going back to Mum.' I said, 'And what about me?' They said, 'We don't know.' So off they went with Mum on the train and left me and the three little ones on our own. I was still a bit shy and although the CWA people were wonderful, the Matron and her staff of two ladies and a man in the yard, I didn't mix. They stayed in their own community and I know they wanted me to go and join with them, but I was too frightened, so I just stayed in my room. I didn't know what to do, my sisters-in-law had gone, and I was worried about what was going to happen to me and my kids. I felt terrible, stranded there on my own.

Darwin was bombed on 19 February 1942. A woman called to tell me and I just stood there thinking 'I wonder if Bill's okay'. I kept my thoughts to myself but they tried to comfort me and help me along. So we stayed there at the CWA. It wasn't a very nice time for me, not knowing if Billy was okay, but I had Harold, Cecilia and the little baby to keep me happy. I gave them hugs and kisses but I really missed being with the Scully family.

After a while we started to itch. Scratch, scratch, scratch. Especially when we took our clothes off. The children and I used to go and sit with the Matron and staff at the dining table, at mealtimes. That's when Matron noticed the kids had blisters on their hands and she said, 'We must take you to see the doctor.' One of the staff took us on the train to the Isolation Hospital. The doctor told me, 'That's scabies. It's contagious. You can't stay where you are or everyone will catch it', and so he sent us to the Brisbane Hospital at Wattlebrae, up on the hill. We had sulphur baths to fix up the scabies but we were lost again; new people in a strange place. I was like a frightened child, but I was learning. I was starting to talk to other people, gradually getting the confidence to make friends. It was the beginning of a small change in me.

Somehow Sarah found out that we were in the hospital and she visited us there. I think she felt guilty for having left us on our own and taking her daughters with her — although this was no fault of hers. When we were discharged she picked us up and took us to her big house in Bowen Hills which had four bedrooms and an attic. Once again, all the Scully family was together again. The children and I lived with them through the early years in Brisbane and Cecilia and then Harold went to school at Fortitude Valley Public School. It was a fair walk and sometimes I caught the local bus and went down to the Valley shopping centre, near the school. All the time I was getting stronger, knowing my way about now, becoming a bit more confident. I reckon I was getting to be a real city-slicker now!

In Brisbane I had to go into the world. I was educating myself about how to survive on my own and it was different from surviving in the Home. Even going to the hospital on the train and talking to strangers, all the nurses and people at the hospital, was a new situation for me. I was even beginning to look people in the face when I talked to them.

At this stage Bill asked the Army to transfer him to Brisbane, so he could see that his wife and three children were getting on okay. The authorities gave him permission and he was with us for just one day. The next day Bill had to leave to join the Second Ninth Battalion that was ready to go to New Guinea to fight the Japanese who had already landed at Milne Bay. The Japanese were planning to take over New Guinea and then move to invade Australia, but they were pushed back at Milne Bay. Fighting still went on in other parts of New Guinea though. When Bill left for New Guinea I was wondering if I was pregnant again. It seemed like every time I saw Billy Muir I ended up pregnant.

Just after Bill left us I was feeling very low but there was a lovely surprise for me. My dear sister Bridget joined us in Brisbane. She had been evacuated a month earlier than me, in December 1941, but by ship. She had four-year-old Shirley and little Bill with her and they'd had to leave in a rush. She'd been told to leave everything, so Bridget was very upset when she arrived. They'd been evacuated so suddenly most of their clothes were still soaking in the wash. A troop ship had become an evacuation ship and it was taking women and children away from danger. The Zealandia was very crowded with Darwin evacuees — both European and Chinese, women and children. As well, they had on board Japanese prisoners of war, a lot of soldiers and the crew. There wasn't much room and they called it a 'hell ship' it was so over-crowded.

Not long after they'd arrived in Brisbane, Bridget's daughter Shirley got diphtheria and was put in the Infectious Hospital where Bridget visited her until she was discharged. Bridget had come and found us in Brisbane but she was lost and frightened, alone in a big city with two little kids, the way I'd been.

So now in that big house we somehow squeezed in Bridget, Shirley and Bill. There were also two old Filipino people there. I don't know where they turned up from, but they lived there with us, too, because Sarah hated to see anyone left out. The old Filipino man was a barber and he cut all our hair for us, while we were living there. It was a bit crowded, but there were no complaints from the neighbours. It was a beautiful house with big gardens. On one side were some lovely people called Hardy. He was a jeweller and his daughter worked with him in the shop.

Living in Brisbane was giving me a whole new outlook. That's why meeting Mrs Roney and Monica was so important for me. They made me feel homesick for Darwin and all our friends there, but I felt stronger, that I could meet up with people and keep in touch.

There wasn't much news in the Brisbane papers or on the radio. The authorities were trying to keep the Darwin bombing a secret so as not to panic people, Sarah reckoned. But the evacuees from Darwin knew something bad was happening because the bush telegraph was still working for us. Some people were getting letters from family who were still there. We were all worried sick, and very sad about the Japanese bombing of Darwin. There were two raids, morning and afternoon, and they killed 243 Europeans but we didn't know how many Aboriginal or Chinese. The Japanese wanted to hit the big oil storage tanks, the ships in the harbour and the wharves, Sarah said. Then, on 20 June 1943, the Japanese really hurt the Scullys. They were bombing the RAAF Base at Winnellie where Sarah and Jim Scully's boy, Private William Scully was stationed at the Shady Glen barracks. He was a member of 29th Australian Employment Company. The raid started, William dropped what he was doing and ran for shelter but it was too late. He was too slow. A bomb exploded and William Scully, my favourite brother-in-law and Billy Muir's favourite brother was dead. Killed by a Japanese bomb they call a daisy cutter. He's buried now at the Adelaide River War Cemetery. Sarah was really upset that her young son was killed like that and we were all crying. She was worried about Joe and the other boys and I worried all the time about Billy Muir in the front line. We were all sad women down there, away from our men. It wasn't like being in Darwin; in Brisbane we were cut off. We were safe living there, but the War still scared us.

It was a big thing for me to go into the middle of Brisbane: all that traffic, cars, buses, trams, trains and taxis. I still felt funny about being looked after by my in-laws. I was hoping to become more independent now that I was more confident. I was ready to live on my own and bring the kids up my way. After all, I had a husband fighting in the War, three children and was an evacuee. Once Bridget was there we wanted to do things on our own and she made me brave enough because she was fun to talk to and we chattered all the time. We decided to find a house for just us. We found an old butcher's shop at Milton that was closed but we went in and asked to rent it. Old Tom Isles who lived there said 'Yeah', so we took it. It had residential rooms upstairs and a kitchen downstairs.

Harold and Cecilia walked down to Milton State School from there. Our children went to school with all the other children and mixed well. There was no colour prejudice and it was a good life.

They had to cross a railway line to get to Milton State School and I used to go with them part of the way, until they met up with other children going to school. One time as the children were coming across the railway bridge one poor girl was killed. That was a busy, busy road.

Bridget and I used to go into town with the children. I'd have a little boy in my arms and people knew we were bush people from the way we looked. One time we were in the city and ready to come home but we were on the wrong side of the street. The kids saw our tram coming but it was going the wrong way. 'Milton,' we said, 'it's going to Milton. That's our tram!' So we tried to catch it, not worrying about the traffic. We ran across the street and got to the wrong side of the tram, the side with a rail on it. We crawled in one by one and luckily there were no cars.

Bridget was there with me for some time in Milton, but John Baird, her husband, was working in Alice Springs with the railways and as there was no bombing in Alice Springs he found a house and wanted his family back. Bridget decided to go back to her husband, but I stayed on at Milton with the kids.

Bill had been away in New Guinea for twenty months, fighting at Milne Bay and on the Kokoda Trail when he came home on two weeks' leave. We were still in Milton, the kids and me, and, of course, he went off again, leaving me pregnant. He went back to New Guinea, to more fighting. After I let him know I was pregnant again he told me to go to the authorities. He said I should tell them I wanted him home to help me with the kids. After all, he'd been on active service all over New Guinea. He wrote to me, 'I want to get out, now. I want to come and try to help you with the kids.' I thought, 'Oh, well. I'll go to Victoria Barracks in Brisbane.' I had to go up a hill, not far from where we were living. I was pregnant and had little Billy walking with me.

'I want to see somebody in charge,' I said. 'I want to see about my husband. He's over in New Guinea and I want him home. He's in action where they're fighting over there but I need him at home to help me. I'm pregnant and I've got these little ones. I'd like it if my husband could get out of the Army and come home to help me.'

'Look here, Madam,' the fellow said. 'You've got these welfare people here that look after you women and children. They're a sort of a home-service, there to help you if you want to go out. Ring these people. Did you know about that?'

I didn't know.

'Well, they will come out and help you.'

I wasn't very happy about that. 'No,' I said. 'I still want my husband home.'

'Look, Madam,' he said. 'It's very hard. Your husband's probably in the front-line. He's a valuable man up there. It's very hard to find your husband and pull him out of the front-line. The whole Army probably wants to come home. No. I'm sorry but it can't be done. He's in action, at the front-line.'

So that was that. I'd tried to get him home.

The next thing, baby James was born on 17 May 1944 in the Brisbane Hospital. So James is a Queenslander. We stayed there in Brisbane at Milton and the people we lived with were lovely old Aboriginal people and I was happy there. They loved me, too, you know. They were caring and showed me a little bit of affection.

9

Back to Darwin

After I couldn't get him out of the Army, Bill wrote to his father, Bob Muir, in the Kimberley. Bill tried to get his father to get him home, by saying he needed help on the land. But there was no way, because he was in action. The Army needed Bill Muir to stay and help win the War. He got knocked back every time, even though he had had malaria on and off the whole time he served in New Guinea.

Before the War ended though, Bill finally did come home. He came to Milton to see us, before he went to Kapooka. He was now an NCO, a non-commissioned officer, and a platoon leader. He was a good soldier, a capable well-liked man. Even when he wasn't in action, Bill was always playing sport or something like that. He hated being still and doing nothing. He'd finished a non-commissioned officer's course and was offered the rank of sergeant but he knocked it back. He didn't want to be above his men, he just wanted the rank of corporal. So they sent him down to Kapooka, an army camp in New South Wales, to train young army cadets. He reckoned those young men got a big shock being told what to do by an Aboriginal man.

The War ended, Bill came to Brisbane, got his discharge in August 1945, and then he went back to Darwin. He got his job back again with Native Affairs and he sent for us straight away. He said to me, 'You and the kids come home. I've got a house and a job.' So we went back to the Territory. Baby Robert was just a month old, I think. I didn't really want to go back to Darwin, even with Billy Muir there. I loved living in Brisbane with my children. It was such a good life with the shops, people I knew, and my new friends. The kids were doing well at school and they had friends there, too. After the freedom of the big city, I didn't like the idea of a small place. But I had no choice: my husband wanted me back in Darwin.

The government supplied an airfare for the children, Molly Anderson and for me because Bill was a returned soldier. All I could do was pack, and say goodbye to the kind old Aboriginal people at Milton who loved us, and the people in the little shop where we bought what we needed.

After four years away, and with my eyes now opened to a new world, Darwin looked and felt strange. The bomb damage was still bad and, after Brisbane, I thought Darwin was really small and shabby. The evacuation had shown me that I could live in a big city.

Sarah Scully stayed on in Brisbane. She came to see us off. When old Jim retired he went there to be with her, but their daughters Gladys and Mona stayed in Brisbane, too. Francesca came back to live in Darwin in 1960.

There were no houses to spare in Darwin. When we got there, I found Bill had been transferred to Delissaville, a settlement for Larrakia people, across the harbour. It's called Belyuen today. You had to get there by boat and Leo Hickey had the contract for going out to the native settlements in his lugger. It was a two-mile journey up a long creek before you reached the landing place. I didn't want to live out there in the bush and I never stopped growling about being there. I was a cityslicker now and I liked the big city with good shops, trams and buses. Delissaville was not what I wanted at all.

During the War, Delissaville was one of the places where Aboriginal men working for the government kept a watch out for Japanese planes or plane crashes. All along the north coast, and on the out-stations and isolated settlements they asked Aboriginal people to keep a look out. The government people called them 'The Black Watch'. Later, I found out this was a European joke.

I felt very isolated when Bill was away working. I had no-one to talk to and I was missing my children who had been put into the Retta Dixon Home. The barge only went into town twice a week. Billy and I put Cecilia, Harold and Billy into the Home otherwise they would have had no schooling. It was nothing like the schooling they could have had in Brisbane. The Retta Dixon Home was now taking the place of the old Kahlin half-caste Home and poor Cecilia, Harold and Billy lived in the government institution for half-caste kids. I was missing my children and was very unhappy and complained until Bill took a transfer back to the mainland to work at the Berrimah Native Reserve, about eight miles out of Darwin.

Living in Brisbane for four years had showed me what life could be for me and the children. I'd enjoyed the shops and met and chatted with people. The children were happy and accepted in school and had friends there, too. Now I was feeling lonely and missing my children.

There were still lots of big army huts round the place, Sidney Williams huts. The Native Affairs people had taken them and put them at Berrimah and Delissaville. So, after four years in civilisation in Brisbane this is where we lived, in a foreman's house on a native settlement with a Superintendent, Tom Wake.

There was no other accommodation available. There were no corner shops for me, no school for the children, no buses or trams and no privacy. I moaned and groaned and let Bill know that I wasn't happy, especially with the children in the Retta Dixon Home, and me not knowing how they were being treated.

I was stuck out at Delissaville with no-one to talk to because Bill left early each morning for work and got home late. He was a truck driver for Native Affairs then, acting as a reserve foreman for Vin White. That's how we'd got the house to live in. I was nearly going crazy with the loneliness. After a while I told Bill, 'Blow that. I'm going to fix it for my children. I want them to go to an ordinary school, along with other kids. I want a proper life and education for them and I want them to be equal. I don't want them feeling they're just half-caste kids, dumped in a home by their Dad and Mum.'

Ours was the last house in the reserve, away from everybody else. It might be quiet and peaceful, but peace and quiet was not what I wanted. I wanted company and a bit of action. This cross woman was not a quiet little thing any more. I was really upset to be back on a reserve with a Superintendent, a long boat trip from town, with no shops or friends and the children in Retta Dixon half-caste Home.

'I can't stand it,' I told Bill one day. 'It's all right for you but I'm not used to this, now, you know. There's been a War on and I'm not a quiet little thing like before. I know what real houses look like, how other people live. I lived four years in Brisbane, in a real city. If I stay here I'll go mad with no proper house, or electricity and water, or people to talk to. All this cooking and washing for all the kids. It's too much.'

So Bill found me someone to help in the house. She was a beautiful old Larrakia woman. She did all the housework and the cooking and looked after Robert who was six-months-old now and crawling around. Dear old Harriet was a lovely old woman. I'd got someone to help me in the house and keep me company but there was one problem. Harriet was deaf and dumb.

So Billy thought he's done a wonderful thing finding someone to help me and keep me company. I reckon Billy Muir just couldn't understand what being lonely was like. There were no convenient things nearby, and no water, so you had to go down the hill to the spring and cart it all the way back up the hill.

After I'd growled for a long time Bill said, 'Okay. We'll go back to town.' Bill got permission for us to live at Berrimah so the kids could come home from the Retta Dixon Home. This was better than living at Delissaville, but it was still nine miles out of town. And each day, away he went to work in town. I was still lonely and Bill was coming home later and later, sometimes well after midnight. He was having a good time at the RSL with his mates, or going to political meetings. I wasn't happy when he came in late and a bit charged up, drunk and wanting dinner after twelve o'clock, seven hours past our proper tea time.

And he was still away a lot because Native Affairs sent him off all the time. I'm not sure how long we stayed at Berrimah but I had one child there and I was young and miserable. I said, 'I don't like this. I want to go into town and live with people. I can't stand this, now. With only children to talk to when they get home from school.'

As a returned serviceman, through the RSL, Bill bought a block of land up near the Japanese graves, Kormilda College and the Berrimah Road, going out to East Arm. I still growled a bit though, because I wanted to be right in town. I said, 'Our kids are good kids. They've got manners and behave properly.' Gradually he began to understand how upset I was. He gave in and said we could come in to town and he began looking for a place around Parap.

In those days few people had motor cars. Before taxis, you just walked if you wanted to go into town. You had to walk. Even when there were taxis, there were no telephones for the public. People who worked for the government had telephones, but no-one we knew.

If I wanted to go to town when Bill was still a truck driver for Native Affairs, he'd come home and give me a lift into town and then back home. I never learnt to drive. I didn't do the food shopping; Bill looked after that. He used to buy mostly meat, potatoes, onions, cabbages, bread, and tea, of course. The milk was condensed or Ideal. Condensed milk, mostly, but sometimes powdered Sunshine milk and butter. There was no electricity, and no fridges, then. We kept things cool in little Coolgardie Safes. A little tin safe with a hollow place on top where you put water that soaked into the cloths hanging down each side of the safe. When the air went through the wet cloths, it made the safe cool. It was never really cold, but it was cooler than outside. Some people living closer to town might have had an icebox but we were too far away to bring the blocks of ice.

In those early years of being married, I was still learning to be a housewife. My place was at home working for my children and husband while Billy worked outside for wages. With the kids coming so fast, there was the washing. Each day I washed, hand washing and boiling a copper. Then I'd do a bit of housework, make the beds, sweep and tidy up the place. I started to cook at about four o'clock, to have dinner ready for my husband.

There was no way of knowing if this was the right thing. Living in the half-caste home and working in a hospital gave me no examples to copy. Sarah Scully was the only model for me in those early days and she only knew the old bush ways. I just sort of picked it up. When we were first married and living with the Scullys we used to cook a big pot of stew and that was main food. You cut up meat, onion, potato and carrot and threw it all in a big pot and boiled it. Sometimes you added a little bit of Holbrooks sauce for flavouring, and thickened it with corn flour or plain flour. That was mostly it.

We ate rice, stew and fried meat. Sometimes Bill wanted something different, a bit of luxury like a rump steak or a T-bone. But mostly it was stew, which was easy and cheaper.

When the children started roaming around, going out with other children and playing Bill wasn't happy. He thought it was an awful thing to come back in to town. I told him I was going off my head living out in the bush. And I wasn't really happy, even at Berrimah. It was still too far from town and other people; a nine-mile walk to get into town, with little kids.

Bill was really trying to find a place for us, but the only place he could find that we could move into was an old shed at Parap. It was a garage next to a house and I think it was the old Parap school house at Stokes Street. They rented us their shed. That's when we moved into an open shed, waiting for them to move out of the house. I was happy to come into town, but the shed was open and not very flash. The kitchen was in the open and I was pregnant again, but happier than at Berrimah. There was one problem: there was only one little room for me and Bill to have privacy.

At one time the baby, Patrick, became sick. He'd probably caught a chill living in the open shed. He must have been sick for about a month but I didn't realise how sick he was. I wasn't well myself and there was nobody I knew enough, or felt safe enough with, to talk to. And there was nobody to take us to hospital. I got gastro, like him, and I must have gone a little cuckoo. I don't know how I looked after the rest of the kids, and then I couldn't move with all the little ones to care for. Patrick died when he was nine months old; it must have been about May 1949. So I said, 'We can't live here. Not now.'

Bill tried to find us a place, but there were no vacancies. We had to wait until somebody moved out. Maybe the kids and I should have stayed in Brisbane, but it was too late now.

10

Flaming furies at Parap Camp

Bill heard there was room for us at Parap Camp, so it was time for us to move house again. During the War, the Parap Camp had been called the 118 Army Camp. Parap was about one and a half miles from Darwin. Living there wasn't too flash, but at least it was closer to town and to people. Our hut was in Eden Street, near the corner of Charles Street.

So we were back to living in a Sidney Willams hut. The huts were just a big open space, like a shed. They had curved tops and were made out of galvanised iron. You had to make your own rooms by partitioning them. We had a bathroom and laundry and a wood stove for cooking which made a lovely fire for cooking toast. The huts had push-out windows that worked well. They gave us a good rush of air through the place and the moving air kept us cool in a humid summer climate.

I can't remember really if it was uncomfortable except for when I was washing for the eleven of us — nine kids plus me and my hubby. There was no shed or anything else for shade and Bill didn't have the time to build me one. He was too busy working, and off drinking with his mates. But I couldn't grumble because life was like that. We were poor and we couldn't afford anything more. But the sun was hot, washing out there every day. With nine kids to wash for, you wash every day and sometimes I was washing at night for school the next day.

There were times when I thought it would kill me, and getting enough wood to run the house was a big problem. The children were sent to collect wood to keep the stove and the copper going. There were no washing machines then, just copper troughs out in the sun for washing and boiling the sheets and towels. You needed wood, too, for cleaning up the lavatory cans. Whatever wood my hubby dropped off went quickly and I had to send the children out looking again. They began to hate the job and soon the trees growing nearby were gone and the kids had to go down into the gully searching for wood. We had no money to buy any.

After a while, it felt like that's all I did. Worry about having enough wood for cooking and washing, and having babies. I liked looking after the children but as soon as I had one another one came along. There wasn't much time between them, just twelve or thirteen months. I don't know how I stood up to all of that. I used to feel sorry for myself but my health stood up through those years. I always had a bad time when I was pregnant, though. I couldn't bend over and my back would be killing me. It was a good thing I liked looking after children.

The older children loved it at Parap Camp. After school when they got home they'd take off and we didn't see them. They just ran around everywhere; down the gully, down to the beach, picking any berries that might be growing. I only saw them when they were hungry and came home for a feed. There were quite a lot of children as most other people had big families too. The children made up their own games or got into little groups with special friends. It was a really happy place, Parap Camp.

That was the best thing about that camp, for me. Not that I had much time to see what my kids were up to because I always had too many little ones to look after. But other people kept a look out, seeing that no-one got hurt if they were fighting, and the kids all took care of one another. There were no fences but it was a good place.

At Parap Camp we all had tin-shed toilets. These had a big tin drum for a toilet pan. Native Affairs didn't send night-cart men or anyone to empty the cans so we had to lower the level, ourselves. We did this by setting fire to them to burn them off. So we needed wood for that too. You put diesel oil in the drum to start it burning and then you put wood in, to keep it going. It would flame away there at night, making a great light all around. That was the thing I remember about Parap Camp: the flaming furies. Sometimes there might be four or five burning at the same time.

After a while half of the drums would get burnt out. There'd be holes around the top and then we'd have to get a new one. The funny thing was that although the fires were quite fierce, I don't remember the little sheds catching fire even though the timber frames sometimes got charred.

The other thing about Parap was the Socials. They had the Sunshine Club, but I didn't have a chance to get along to the club nights because I had too much to do at home. They used to have a dance once a week and it was a nice time to go out and dress up and dance. I stayed home, but I was happier at Parap Camp than at Berrimah or Delissaville because I had people around me for company.

Mr Anderson and Mrs Anderson, who I'd been evacuated to Brisbane with, lived next door, Mrs Ellen Morrison was across the road and there were the Fejos, Alice and Sammy. Mostly we kept to ourselves, with only a few friends, but Ellen Morrison was someone else we got on well with. I didn't really have time to go visiting, and anyway, I wasn't one for going next door and sitting down. I had nine children at home and washing and cooking was enough for me. I had no social life and no time. There were a lot of people there with big families. The Angeles, Lew Fatts, Cubillos. Then the Muirs and the Talbots. Mr and Mrs Charlie

Talbot had a big family. But the Muirs, the Cubillos and the Angeles, we had more than the others. We all had either eight or ten children each.

I think because there were so many children at Parap Camp the authorities decided they should get a preschool going. They brought in a lady from down south to be the Director. She was Miss Joyce Gilbert and she came through either Welfare or Native Affairs.

The authorities came out to Parap Camp and called a meeting. This was to see if people wanted to start a preschool child-minding centre. At this time, my cousin, Babe Damaso, was with Native Affairs and he went around asking everyone if they wanted to come to the meeting and that's how I got involved. My youngest, Isabel, was six-years-old by this time, so the idea was too late for me, but I thought it could be good for others.

A lot of people weren't too happy for their children to be sent to a centre. The mothers quite liked keeping their little children at home with them. They felt funny about letting the government, or strangers, look after their little kids all day, and that's how I felt too.

But then my cousin Babe asked me to go around with another lady, Mrs Tanni Bennett and I began to see how it might be a good idea. We talked to the mothers and told them how it would be good for the children, doing things like painting and playing before they went to school. They would have little swings in their playground and things like that, and there'd be a fence so the kids couldn't run off. We told them that the children wouldn't play on their own, but would be supervised by a couple of ladies, special pre school teachers, who'd be in charge.

Then we got to have a big laugh. The first thing the government asked was if we could put some money in to run the place. They said we could raise money with socials and raffles. So Mrs Tanni Bennet said she'd hold a card game at her place, and then I could have one.

And that's what we did. First she'd have a card game and then me, right at the other end of the place. Each time, we'd collect some 'tong' out of it. That's what Darwin people call it; I don't know what term white people use. You'd put money in a small box. It was really just a little money box kept for a special purpose. Perhaps it's a Chinese word, or something like that.

We all collected money and it must have been a fair bit, because the government was pleased that we were so keen. The school was in Charles Street where there was an empty Sidney Williams hut and it was next to the Anglican Church hut.

After a while a few people started sending their children, and then the other mothers realised that it was a good idea, keeping the children together playing, and with somebody looking after them, supervising. It gave all the mothers a bit of free time for a change and with the children safely looked after, the mothers could relax.

I stayed there and worked at the centre, cleaning and helping, and getting a small payment. It wasn't very much but it was a little bit of money for me, so that was very handy. Later there was a meeting and they wanted to elect somebody onto the advisory board and I was elected to represent my people. I said to Miss Gilbert, 'But I don't know what to say. I've never been mixed up in anything like this before. What do I do?' Miss Gilbert told me not to worry. She said I wouldn't have to speak or anything like that, and if there was a vote she'd help me.

There was a man there from the ABC and he was on the Advisory Board too. I didn't know anything about meetings and I was worried about how it was going to involve me. But I went along to the Board meeting and I didn't have to do anything. Mr Giese, the Director, was there and he chaired the meeting.

This must have been about 1957 because Isabel, my youngest, was about six or seven. The centre became really popular as people realised how good it was for kids and mothers to have this place to send their kids. More and more people started sending their kids there and so I became involved in community politics. It was the first time for me, but Bill had been involved in politics before, when he was just a young man.

In 1956 Bill Muir, Babe Damaso, Jack McGinness, Timmy Angeles, Sheila Clark and other people living in Parap Camp, set up a group called the Northern Territory half-castes Association. They asked the federal government to give them full citizenship rights, but all Canberra did was make changes to the Aboriginal Ordinance (NT), exempting some people from the restrictions from buying alcohol.

After the War, the ex-servicemen decided to work for even more changes. Their experiences in the armed forces gave them a different attitude to their treatment by the authorities. At about this time, the government decided that they would stop calling us Aboriginal or half-caste and that we would be called coloured. In the Parap Camp, in about 1950, Bill got involved again with Northern Territory half-castes Association, just as he had in the Union movement with Grandpa Jim Scully in 1936, before we were married. So Billy Muir got involved with politics again; this time half-caste and human rights and even the way ex-servicemen were treated by the authorities. This time, Jack McGinness was running the show and Bill and other members had lots of meetings to attend.

Bill and the other half-caste ex-servicemen, were very upset at the way the authorities let them serve in the Army and fight for their country, but after the War they still couldn't buy grog in pubs. It seemed you were reliable enough to be a corporal, in charge of men in New Guinea and training young cadets at Kapooka, but when the War was over and the Army didn't need you any more, the authorities said the law could go back to the way it was before. The half-caste ex-servicemen wanted full citizenship and human rights! They wanted to be able to walk on the same footpath as whites. This is what the Northern Territory half-castes Association was about. Bill felt that if he was responsible enough to fight in the War, and train young white cadets, he should be good enough to go into a pub and buy a beer for himself and his white mates after the War. They sent delegations to Canberra to change the laws and get a bit of equality round the place.

Bill was always coming home late after the meetings, but I was happier in Parap Camp than before. I had people to talk to, all the children were with us at home, and I got involved helping with the preschool kindergarten.

In 1960 land was being released for people to buy and build their own houses. There was a block out at Fanny Bay in McColl Street reserved for ex-servicemen. Two men were after it but it was decided by the ex-service people that Bill should have it because he had more children than the other chap, even though some of ours had grown up and moved away. Now we had our block of land and Bill got a War Service loan to build a house.

We needed to find a builder. Our block was big, nearly two acres and it was long and wide in front. Bill found a builder and the home was erected on very high stilts, nearly nine feet off the ground. I think Bill always had in mind to build rooms underneath.

It had a timber-frame house built on stilts, with glass louvre windows — an ordinary Darwin house. We had a big kitchen, a bathroom, a few bedrooms and a big living room. Nobody ever had a sitting room. We bought beds, a big kitchen table, kitchen chairs, a few cupboards and folding canvas chairs. That was the only furniture we could buy in those times. But canvas chairs were common then and they were very comfortable and cool for sitting around in.

Finally we moved into our house in McColl Street, Fanny Bay. Now we were living closer to the shops and other people. After all this time I felt happier, living back in Darwin. It only took us fourteen years to get a place near the shops and other people, and near a school for the children!

When we left Parap Camp, I stopped working for the preschool centre. After a while Miss Gilbert became sick and had to go south. Mrs Tanni Bennet and I weren't asked to her farewell party and we felt hurt about that after we'd done so much to get the school started. We didn't get a chance to say goodbye to Miss Gilbert, or to keep in touch.

Hilda and Billy Muir on their wedding day, 1940.

His Honour the Administrator.

W. Muir - Return of Wife and Children to the Northern Territory

        W. Muir, truck-driver employed by this Branch, is a half-caste. His wife and four children under 10 years of age, were compulsorily evacuated from the Northern Territory and are at present residing in Brisbane, they now desire to return to Darwin.

        Your approval is sought for the grant of steamer fares to them for the journey Brisbane to Darwin.

        Muir was one of the few half-castes in the Northern Territory who saw active service outside of Australia; his record includes actual battle service at Milne Bay, Buna, Finchshaven and Bouganville. Major McCaffery of the Police Force, when visiting Darwin recently, informed me that Muir had the reputation of being a good soldier, so much so that he desired to meet him here in Darwin.

        Although Muir is not a permanent officer I consider that he should be granted assistance in having his family returned to Darwin.

        Submitted.

(V.J. White)
Chief Clerk

Native Affairs,
Darwin,
1st April, 1946.

Native Affairs' 1946 request to the Administrator for assistance with fares for Billy, Hilda and family to move back to Darwin from Brisbane.

Hilda and Billy Muir on their wedding day, 1940.

His Honour the Administrator.

W. Muir - Return of Wife and Children to the Northern Territory

W. Muir, truck-driver employed by this Branch, is a half-caste. His wife and four children under 10 years of age, were compulsorily evacuated from the Northern Territory and are at present residing in Brisbane, they now desire to return to Darwin.

Your approval is sought for the grant of steamer fares to them for the journey Brisbane to Darwin.

Muir was one of the few half-castes in the Northern Territory who saw active service outside of Australia; his record includes actual battle service at Milne Bay, Buna, Finchshaven and Bouganville. Major McCaffery of the Police Force, when visiting Darwin recently, informed me that Muir had the reputation of being a good soldier, so much so that he desired to meet him here in Darwin.

Although Muir is not a permanent officer I consider that he should be granted assistance in having his family returned to Darwin.

Submitted.

(V.J. White)
Chief Clerk

Native Affairs,
Darwin,
1st April, 1946.

Native Affairs' 1946 request to the Administrator for assistance with fares for Billy, Hilda and family to move back to Darwin from Brisbane.

GJW   43/60   30th August, 1946

The Chief Clerk,
Department of the Interior,
CANBERRA.   A.C.T.

MRS. HILDA JOYCE MUIR AND FIVE CHILDREN -
APPLICATION FOR ASSISTANCE TO RETURN TO DARWIN.

In reply to your Memorandum dated 23rd August, 1946, 46/2/19
the Native Affairs Branch states that approval has already
been granted for the Administration to bear the cost of
the return fares of Mrs. Muir and her children.

The husband is employed as a truck driver at Delissaville
and in his spare time has erected a house.

It is suggested that the Department of Social Services
be advised that Mr. Muir has adequate accommodation for his
wife and children and that arrangements for their return
to Darwin may be made as soon as a favourable opportunity
presents itself.

(L.H.A. GILES)
Government Secretary.

Approval given to Native Affairs in 1946 for assistance
with fares.

Hilda with children in Brisbane during World War II, (*left to right*) Cecilia, Harold and baby Billy.

Hilda with children in Darwin during the 1950s, (*left to right*) Alan, Isabel, Thomas and Jean.

Harry Gore, Hilda's eldest brother.

Clockwise from top left, Bernie Talbot (friend) Bill Jnr, Robert and James Muir.

(*Left to right*) Tom Dare, Robert, Jean, Isabel, James, Alan, Bill, Hilda and Thomas at home in Fannie Bay, 1963.

Billy and Hilda Muir at daughter Jean's wedding, 1972.

Hilda, on trip back to Borroloola, 2000.

Hilda with sister Jessie, and her daughter
Ivy and three grandchildren on the trip
back to Borroloola, 1973.

Borroloola Centenary celebrations in 1988. *Left to right*, Hilda, Connie Bush, Ian Tuxworth (Member for Barkly), Rita Cottrel, Ruth Vincent and Evelyn Baird.

Hilda with (*left to right*) Sir William Deane, Evelyn Baird, Lady Helen Deane and Judy Friel.

Hilda *(seated, third from right)* with her Borroloola family during the Land Court hearing for Yanuwa country, 2000.

Hilda taking part in the ceremony that welcomed the Land Court hearing.

Court hearing for Yanuwa country held on Kangaroo Island with Judge Olney (*seated in middle*).

Hilda going fishing with younger members of her Borroloola family on Kangaroo Island.

Hilda sitting beside a canoe outside the old police station (now a museum) in Borroloola, 2000.

Hilda with Clare Anderson (*middle*) and Clare Brown who travelled with Hilda on horseback in 1928.

Hilda with Alec Kruger at the High Court in Melbourne.
(Photo courtesy of Ponch Hawkes)

Between Two Worlds conference in Canberra. (*Left to right, seated*)
Emily Liddle, Hilda and Daisy Ruddick with (*standing*) Ruby Hunter
and Archie Roach.

11

Cyclone Tracy — Floorboards lifting

When we'd been living in our house at Fanny Bay for a while I got work with the Arafura Hostel. It was a cleaning job and it gave me some income again, so Bill could do what he liked with his. By this time, Bill had bought an old tray-top truck and sometimes we went to the pictures, or he'd take us all for trips down the bitumen, to Pine Creek and Batchelor. We went for picnics out in the bush and this is what Bill liked best. By this time Bill had become a lot quieter and he seemed to be home earlier. He wasn't running round so much. He was still grogging a bit but he seemed more settled than before.

I worked for the hostel for the next nine years. In the early 1970s Bill was working with the railways, and he was always coming home and telling me how he and his mate, Otto, an Italian man, were going overseas for a holiday. There was another old chap too, Albert, also Italian. Bill said he and Otto were going to take Albert to Italy, or overseas for a holiday. He was happy and excited.

'True,' I said. 'What about me?'
'No. Only the men are going.'

'But you and I are supposed to stick together. What's the matter with me?' I said.

'Otto said it was only for men,' he told me.

'I know what you're going for,' I said. 'Oh well. That's you, going to go overseas,' I said.

You know what they're like when they've been drinking a bit.

At the same time I'd heard about some people from the Royal Darwin Hospital booking to go on a cruise ship. There were about six of my mates from work. I said to Bill, 'Oh well. If you think you can just go and have a good time, I'm going to book on this trip with those other Aboriginal women. If you're going overseas by yourself, then I might book on this ship and go myself.' And I did. I went in to the Sitmar Office and booked a trip on the Fairstar, leaving Darwin for a cruise on 15 April 1975. Poor old Billy was always coming out with things just to make me jealous. And I did it just for the devilment, you know. To show him.

So the next week, on payday, I began putting money away. I was determined to go on the trip with those other Darwin people. Each payday I paid a bit more off my ticket. That was the last I heard of Bill's trip. I think what he'd said about going to Europe was just the grog talking, to upset me. But soon something happened to change all that silly business. Something to really make me upset.

In Darwin, late in the year, the cyclone season comes. On Christmas Eve in 1974 I was working at the Arafura Hostel. We knocked off at about three o'clock and that's when the wind started to get strong. The day was steaming hot, you could hardly breathe and the cyclone warning was out. Before the Christmas Eve cyclone, there was supposed to have been another one. Early in December it came and they gave out warnings, but then it blew out. Then it happened again with cyclone two. So that was two cyclones that had just come and blown out, and here was the third cyclone warning. The wind started on 21 December and by Christmas Eve it was getting stronger. We got a third warning about the cyclone: to tie everything down and make sure it was secure. But people were saying, 'Oh, we've heard that twice now, and they both blew out'. And so we thought this next cyclone, the third, was going to be the same. It would come and then blow out. But we were wrong.

The third cyclone was like a demon. There were clouds, thick like smoke, coming over, and before these clouds rolled in, lots of ducks and geese flew over in formation, going south for safety. Millions of ants were on the run as well. I believe some bush Aboriginal people warned the authorities that there was going to be a big storm. They could tell, from the birds. A lot of Aboriginal people went down the track, out of Darwin. They saw the real warning, just before the big black clouds came rolling in over the Arafura Sea. My mate Cathy and I saw the birds when we came out of the Hostel. All those birds, but we didn't read the sign, we didn't know.

The sky was black now. You've never seen anything like it. It was three o'clock, time for us to knock off; time to do a bit of shopping on Christmas Eve. I went home but nobody was there. At about four o'clock my daughter Cecilia and her children came in. I don't know where they'd been, but they came to visit. The wind was getting stronger. It must have been about five o'clock when Bill came home.

I was surprised to see him. He hadn't gone to work that day because Cecilia and the children had just come back from Adelaide and Bill had decided to take the day off. He was going to borrow some money from Custom Credit so he could help buy a few bits of furniture for them as they'd come back with nothing.

He'd been in town all day, doing his thing, shopping or at the RSL Club as usual, or going to borrow money. He'd agreed to get a loan for $500 for the furniture. He was really exhausted when he came in, and as he'd brought a few beers home he just went straight to bed. That's the first time that Bill didn't celebrate Christmas Eve.

Cecilia and the four kids were there: Maria, Inez, Francesca and Petra, and a school friend from the Adelaide boarding school,

Pilawuk. Bill was asleep and I was reading to the kids. At about seven or eight o'clock, the wind was still getting stronger and Isabel and her little baby boy, Brenton, came in. Cecilia decided to go home to her new house; one 'on the ground' in a newish housing development, built when they were opening up suburbs at Nightcliff, Ludmilla, Milner and Rapid Creek, where the old Bagot Reserve used to be. She asked if Bill and I wanted to go there, away from our 'upstairs' house. I said 'I don't know. I'll go and ask Dad.' So I woke Bill up and said, 'The children are ready to go home. Cecilia wants to know if we can go to that house, get away from Fanny Bay.'

He woke up a bit and said, 'Oh no. I'm not coming. You can go, you and Isabel, and the baby. You go. I'll be all right.'

So I came back and told Cecilia, 'No. Dad's too tired; he's exhausted. I can't leave him, so you and the kids go. I've got to stay with Dad.'

Isabel drove Cecilia and her children home, leaving little Brenton with us, asleep. Then Isabel came back and stayed with us and the little baby. Billy Muir slept on and on.

He'd had no drink, nothing on Christmas Eve. It was the first time in forty years that Bill hadn't celebrated Christmas Eve. What was going on here? What was wrong with Billy Muir? At about half past ten things were getting really scary. The glass-panelled front door flew open, smashing against the wall and sending glass everywhere and suddenly, the cyclone was in the house. This was a bad moment; as if we knew something awful was going to happen.

I could hardly breathe with the fright. It was as if there was a madman outside with a great hammer, going round and smashing all the louvres in. As if, all of a sudden, your life in this house wasn't safe anymore. With your front door smashed and the windows gone, there was nothing to keep out anyone or anything. It was a frightening feeling.

I raced in to Billy and shook him, yelling, 'Come on now. Wake up. This is serious. Things are smashing all around us'. You couldn't walk into the kitchen which was taking the force of the wind but the bedroom was down at the calm end of the house. We had a fancy door with a glass window but it smashed easily and broke into pieces on the kitchen floor.

Billy jumped out of bed, grabbed Isabel and me and the baby and threw us all in the narrow passage between the bathroom and the toilet, away from the splintering glass. I went and grabbed a warm jacket just to wrap around the baby. I had nothing else for this little boy, just six months old. The wind was blowing at the bathroom window and then that smashed too. The door was banging but Bill couldn't shut it because the wind was too strong. We managed to shelter a bit in the passage way but the next minute there was a terrible noise as the bathtub dropped, straight to the ground below. The bath had been sucked out of the house.

Then the electricity went off and we were in darkness except for the great flashes of lightning that kept the sky all silver and jagged. But we could hardly see the lightning, because we were too scared to take our hands from our faces. The rain was teeming down and we crouched there, soaking wet and deafened by the sound of the terrible wind. That wind pounded at us, blowing across the sea from Casuarina. The bathroom door kept banging, like a warning that we too could be sucked out, down to the ground. But no. Somehow, that sheltered corner protected us from getting sucked through the hole. Isabel and I half sat, half crouched on the floor, with the baby Brenton between us. Bill was sort of hovering over us, using his big, strong body as a roof.

I only had a nightdress on and Bill had a pair of shorts. I don't know if he even had a shirt on. The rain was pouring in on us, coming down in buckets as if it wanted to drown us. The whole house was shuddering and creaking as if the wind was a screaming demon trying to get in to kill us, as if it had hold of our little house and was shaking it like a piece of paper, seeing if we'd all fall out, or if the house would tumble over. Rain was flooding into the house through the broken windows and the blown-in door. We crouched there, praying, 'Please God, save the baby'. I said it over and over.

We were all in a state of shock, that a cyclone could come to Darwin like this when two other two cyclones had just fizzled out.

I didn't know what time it was, perhaps midnight or one or two o'clock. After a while, it felt like we'd been there forever, numb with terror and exhaustion. Suddenly, the wind got slower, quieter. There seemed to be one great flash of lightening and then the wind just stopped, as if someone had shut a big door somewhere; had cut off the wind and the noise.

We waited a bit and then Bill stood up and said, 'That might be it'. I followed him down the stairs and into the garden, leaving Isabel and Brenton inside. There was still sheet lightning, making it almost as bright as day, but the sky was heavy with great clouds. It was dark but sort of glowing. It was really eerie and scary. We saw bits of wood and iron all over the lawn. There were bits of other people's houses too, but I don't think we knew what they were.

The trees in our yard had been flattened. There were no leaves left on the branches and the bushes were all gone too. But Isabel's car was still parked in the driveway and the old caravan was safe in the corner of the yard. The old Malay man who lived in it was safe, too. I still remember how bright it was; like a full moon.

We'd just begun to relax and breathe again when the wind came back, but this time from the other direction. We'd been thinking 'Oh, that's good. It's over.' We didn't understand about the eye of the cyclone so we were walking around outside just as the wind came roaring again. It was like standing right behind a mob of planes starting up. I got such a fright, my heart nearly stopped. Bill was yelling and pushing me up the stairs and down the little passage by the toilet, yelling at Isabel to come. We threw ourselves down again, in the rain and pools of water, while the lightning lit up everything. Billy Muir arched his body over us again. And we stayed there, all huddled up, with the little fellow in the middle.

Our block had no shelter from the wind. There was a big open park and only a few trees and shrubs. Then there was the Georges Crescent side, behind the park, and then the Fanny Bay Esplanade.

For the rest of night we prayed to the dear Lord, praying for Brenton, mostly. 'Please God, save Brenton. Save this little man.' I didn't pray for poor old Bill or Isabel. All I asked God to save was this little fellow. This six-month-old grandson of mine. Isabel was just a small girl and she was there with me, with Bill stretched over us as we huddled there. I don't know how long but it must have been a terrible strain for him. He may have been really scared, too, but he didn't let on. When the eye of the storm passed we heard a big explosion. I reckon those two other cyclones must have all got together, got married and boom, made a big explosion. It was like the Hiroshima bomb or something, all around us. The rain was back now, worse than ever, and still we had the lightning. The wind was roaring, screaming at us from across the open park. With no windbreak at all, it seemed stronger than ever. That's when I felt real despair.

The wind was getting stronger, the floor was getting looser and in the next minute I felt real fear: we could feel the floor lifting. The big bolts that screwed the floor to the piers started lifting. You could hear them being ripped out by the force of the wind as the floor lifted. It was a good solid house but not strong enough against this demon wind blowing in from the Arafura Sea. It was worst when we felt the whole house — the floor and the walls — being blown away from all around us. The timber started breaking and falling on top of us and that was it. My heart was in my mouth and I felt like my ears were going to burst my fear was so great. After that I was just out of it. I don't know how long I was unconscious before I came to, lying on the ground with the house smashed all around me.

It was towards daybreak when I came around. I thought, 'Oh gosh, I'm injured but I'm going to try to get help.' I still had the baby in my arms when I woke up and I felt my back resting on something, maybe the floor, but I had the baby and I wouldn't let go of him.

Isabel must have come to at nearly the same time. She came over to see the baby. I said, 'I'm hurt. I'm going to look for somebody to help me. You take the baby.' The poor girl took her little son, even with her arm broken. She took him to her Dad. I was in deep shock. I watched Isabel take the baby from me and lie him next to his grandfather on the lawn. I wasn't worrying about Bill, even then. It felt like a dream as I watched my daughter take her baby from me and lie him next to his grandfather. Billy Muir just lay there with his little grandson beside him. I saw them both, but I didn't feel anything, it was as if I no longer had the capacity to feel, that the wind had sucked out my emotions.

I said, 'I'm going down the road to see if somebody can help me.' Isabel went with me next door to the Chinese people.

'Harry, can you help us? We'd like to get to the hospital,' I said.

'Sorry. I can't help you,' he replied, dazed and confused. We were all in shock. His house looked okay though — it was really strongly built.

Isabel let go of my arm. 'I'm going back to Dad and baby,' she said.

'All right. You go back,' I said.

I went from where she left me to the neighbours across the yard, but they couldn't help. I started to feel really strange, fuzzy in the head. I got onto my hands and knees and crawled through the fence into Banyan Street. There was a young man who said, 'Sorry, I can't help you.' So I had to crawl through the fence to the next street, Hinkler Crescent, where Phoebe McQuinn was.

Phoebe's family lived in a Sidney Williams hut with an all-steel construction and it was cemented in. When the cyclone started she went there with her children and they were safe. In a stupor, I stood up and walked towards Phoebe. As soon as she saw me she got a rug, wrapped it around me and took me inside. I must have looked a sight. Like an injured half-drowned rat, I reckon. I had a badly gashed head, and a fractured skull and ribs. Of course at that stage I didn't know what was wrong with me. I only knew that I felt awful, sick, and that I wanted to see a doctor.

Phoebe put me in her car and drove me to the Darwin hospital. I'm still thankful to her today for helping me. I didn't really notice anything much as we went. I was so exhausted and in deep shock that I didn't notice that most of Darwin had been blown away. So it wasn't just Billy and Hilda's house that had gone. Most of the other houses had gone, too. And all the trees and bushes.

Looking back on it now I feel really bad that I really only worried about getting to the hospital and not about Isabel, the baby or Billy. This was really strange because for all our lives together, since I'd first met Billy, he'd been the number one for me. I'd always looked after him first, and now all I could think of was Hilda, as number one. Not even my grandson, who I prayed for so hard during the storm. In survival, all I could do was worry about myself. I was in deep shock.

They put me in a wheelchair and Phoebe left me there at the hospital, in the care of the nursing staff. Later someone brought in my daughter Isabel and the little baby.

'Your daughter just came in,' somebody told me.

'Where's Dad?'

'He's in the next ward.'

'Oh. That's all right.'

Then James and Cecilia came in and saw me.

I asked again, 'Where's Dad?'

'Oh. Dad's all right, he's in the next ward.'

I didn't know, then, that Billy Muir was already dead. Or maybe dying right then, no-one told me because they were scared because of the state I was in. Well. That's it. But the funny thing is that my bed was next to the window and a small black bird came pecking at my window. It was as if he was looking at me, pecking on the glass. I don't know if it's true that they come to tell you that there's bad news for you.

They evacuated Isabel, little Brenton and me to Brisbane on an RAAF plane as they did other injured people. I had seven broken ribs, a fractured jaw, a fractured skull and gashed head. Isabel had broken the lower part of her arm and little Brenton had a broken arm too.

I was in Brisbane, sitting and thinking and Isabel was there. She could walk around all right and we were in the same ward.

'Where's Dad?' I asked her.

'He's somewhere in the hospital,' she answered.

It must have been the second day we were there when my eldest son, Harold, came in to visit us. He'd been living in Brisbane with his family, which is what he'd wanted ever since he was evacuated as a wartime child.

'Well, Mum, I've got to tell you. I've got to tell you that Dad died in the cyclone,' he told me.

I threw myself back and howled. The poor old bloke.

'They wouldn't tell you straight away,' he said. He just came out and said it, but not in a sad way, 'Dad died in the cyclone.' And that's it.

I screamed through that whole hospital. I couldn't believe that my beautiful strong Billy Muir was gone. That I had taken myself to the hospital not being able to worry about Isabel and the baby and poor Billy Muir, not even walking over to look at him lying there on the lawn; I didn't even take a last look or say goodbye.

So Bill died on Christmas Day 1974, without celebrating Christmas Eve with his mates in the RSL. I don't know why he came home to us on Christmas Eve, or why he was so tired. But he'd been there, to protect his wife, his youngest daughter and his smallest grandchild with his body, all through that awful night. So, for that, I loved him even more.

I think that's why I had such a bad nervous reaction, later on. I'd never had the chance to say goodbye. By the time I knew he was gone forever, he'd been buried, so I didn't even get a chance to say goodbye at the funeral. Saying goodbye is important for people. People the world over have ceremonies: Aboriginal nations, European nations and Asian nations, all have ceremonies for saying goodbye. You have to deal with death and then you can face it. But that didn't happen with me. I didn't get the chance to resolve our life together. There was no healing recognition of all we'd been through.

After the cyclone I lay in Brisbane Hospital thinking about Billy Muir. Thinking about how he stayed there all night with me and with Isabel and Brenton, not running around or drinking with his mates at the RSL. How he'd got the loan for the furniture for Cecilia and her children in their new house. Thinking how, after all his grogging on, coming home happy at all hours, charged up, sometimes being too tough on the kids, hurting me, running round with other women, being a real goodtime man, he'd come good. His big strong arms had been around me, just like the first time. Only this time we'd been frightened, fighting for our lives. But right at the end, Billy Muir was there with me. And me with him. At the end, in our last big fight with life, we were together, and he was there for me when he was needed.

12

Nerve trouble

After a while I had just a bandage around my head to keep my broken jaw firm. I recovered in January and February. I was getting stronger during March and the Fairstar trip was due in April.

My name was down, so I continued putting something more aside and saving. I was beginning to get around all right when I got a card from Gail Fitzgerald at the Arafura Hostel. She said, 'Hilda, if you're well enough to go on that cruise, then go.' This gave me a bit of encouragement, reminding me that I was getting strong. Gradually I paid more off my fare and on 14 April 1975 the ship came to Brisbane. I was thinking Darwin people would be on it so I asked at the office, but they said, 'We don't know. Find out when you get on board.'

My son-in-law helped me carry my luggage and the children and the girls in Brisbane were all invited too, to come and look around the boat. When I got on the ship there was no-one I knew from Darwin as a result of Cyclone Tracy. Some people had no money to keep paying for their tickets, while others were too injured to travel. I was excited and happy to be going somewhere by myself and with the prospect of being among new people. I still wondered about what had happened to those other Aboriginal ladies who had booked the trip with me.

We boarded the ship at Hamilton Wharf in the Brisbane River. We went out from Brisbane right through to Noumea but we didn't stop there. The first port of call was Port Vila, then Vanuatu, Laetoka, Suva, Bora Bora, Tahiti, Pago Pago and the New Hebrides. Ten islands, I think with two or three days in each port. Then across to New Zealand, and finally back to Sydney.

When I got to my cabin I found I was sharing it with a white woman, about my age. She seemed quite nice at first and we got on well together. But as the cruise went on, it was obvious this old lady used to like her drink a bit. I only drink a little, I'm a really small-time social drinker. I'm just as happy to have tea or water, or a soft drink. Anyway, we got into arguments when we got to New Zealand. She thought she was my boss and that I had to do everything her way. I started making friends with anyone and everyone, and she didn't like that. I think she was jealous, the silly old thing. I think she thought she owned me and that I couldn't manage by myself.

We were walking down a street in Auckland and she was collecting different vegetable seeds. I wanted to go to the post office. 'No,' she said. 'You come with me.' I wanted to send a telegram home, to let my family know that I'd arrived in Auckland and was fine. She repeated, 'You come with me.' I got impatient and we start screaming at each other in the street. Just as well the wharf wasn't too far from where we were. I said, 'Off you go, Kath, I'll find my way.'

I went over to the post office and I met some other people, Christian people. I said, 'I'm from Darwin.' The lady and her daughter said they had a friend in Darwin and she turned out to be my niece, Ruth!

'I'm so happy to meet you. I just had a bit of an incident with my friend,' I told them.

They helped me send my telegram and I found my way back

Very Big Journey

to the ship because it wasn't too far. I just ignored Kath after that. I was cross and hurt by her, but I wasn't going to let her spoil my first trip. I was independent.

When the ship pulled in to Sydney Harbour at the end of the trip, the wharfies were on strike. You should have seen the poor crew of the ship trying to move the baggage. This was the first time we had to go through Customs. I saw Kath with a group of friends and they were all having a big party; she'd just let her head go and was drinking with her friends. She was drunk and you should have seen the poor old thing trying to manage with that bit of a bad limp and all that baggage. The Customs people emptied out her case and went through it when she told them she was bringing in seeds.

As I went past her, I said, 'Kath, you have to look after yourself.'

On that trip I met many good people I kept in touch with for a long time afterwards. This was the start of a new life for me. I really took to travelling. There was laughter and happiness. My first cruise really took my mind off the fear and sorrow I'd suffered during the cyclone. It helped me start a new life without Bill. This was the first time in my whole life that I'd left Australia. It was like my time in Brisbane after being evacuated. I was meeting new people and finding that coming from the Kahlin Home wasn't a big problem. My new friends from the cruise were all white people.

Isabel and I stayed in Sydney for a couple of nights after the cruise finished and then we flew to Brisbane where we stayed for nearly twelve months. It seemed like nearly half my family was in Brisbane. Having lived there during the War and then as a result of our evacuation after the cyclone, Brisbane was like a second home to me. It was a lovely feeling. I had Isabel and little Brenton there, Harold and his family, Robert and his girlfriend, as well as Sarah Scully and her daughters. Living there felt natural and happy. It felt like old times when I was younger, in one big family.

I kept thinking that I didn't want to go back to Darwin. I was angry at what had happened. I'd lost Bill and I couldn't see what there was to go back to. It seemed sad to go back, to the memories with the empty block, the house and everything I'd last had with Bill gone. Gradually I got over that first fear and sadness, and the anger about not being able to say goodbye to Bill and missing his funeral. Then Isabel said she'd like to go back to Darwin, so we started to think about it.

After the cyclone, on Boxing Day, Cecilia and her kids had been evacuated to Brisbane because the authorities wanted everyone out of Darwin. In Brisbane, they put the evacuated people at Enoggerah Army Camp. Then, when the Army wanted to come back to camp, the evacuees had to move out. Early in 1976 they were flown to Adelaide and put into the Pennington Hostel, near Port Adelaide. Cecilia chose to go to Adelaide and she put her two older girls back in the Cabra Convent boarding school. When she was there she joined some of her Darwin friends, studying at the Aboriginal Task Force at the South Australian Institute of Technology. They all signed up to do social work and community development. They wanted to get a proper education so they could get better jobs than their mothers who were working as domestics.

My daughter Jeanie took over Cecilia's old house in Ryland Road, Rapid Creek, so that's where Isabel and I went when we got back to Darwin in June 1976. It was a really funny feeling being back in Darwin without Bill. For all those years Bill had worked all over that town. He was part of the Darwin scene and it just didn't feel right being there alone without him. I always had the feeling that he might come in at any minute.

Those last years before the cyclone Bill had been getting older, mellowing. He seemed to be drinking less, staying home a bit more and he was more content than he'd ever been. He wasn't as restless.

We'd been getting on better when we were alone together. He was always hard on the children when they were growing up, especially the boys. It used to upset me, so we'd argue. It was better when they'd grown up and moved out of the family home. By the end, though, he loved being a father who sent money to his children to show them their Dad still loved them very much.

    Not long after I got back to Darwin I started to have trouble with my nerves, as if they were playing up or something. That's when I began to have my breakdown. It was as if all the bad thoughts and feelings had been waiting for me until I got back to Darwin. First my blood pressure went sky high and the doctor told me to stay at home. Then I feared being away from the house so the district nurses came to visit me. I was on pills for high blood pressure and the nurses used to come to see that I was taking my pills properly. But my blood pressure used to soar when anyone, even the nurses, came to visit. I was scared and didn't want to talk to anybody. It sounds silly, but I couldn't help it. I used to go and bury myself in my room. Panic attacks, that's what they called it.

    I changed from seeing my local doctor to seeing one in Ward One at Darwin Hospital. This was the ward for the cyclone breakdown cases and it was a busy place then.

    I had an appointment to see the doctor and I remember somebody coming in, bleeding, from an accident. I was frightened and tried to run away. I didn't want to see this ugly thing. A friend of mine was there with me and she said, 'Aunty, pull yourself together. Don't be like that.' She was trying to reassure me. 'Come on now, Aunty. Don't be like that. Don't be frightened.'

    I said, 'That's all right for you to say that but I can't help it.' I started shaking again.

    At Darwin hospital I tried to tell the doctor my story. I just loved this kind, gentle man. He said, 'Oh well. I'll register you in the hospital.' This man took pity on me because I was in a bad way. I was taking my blood pressure medicine, but I wasn't getting better. I was just still going through that panic period when I couldn't stand anybody coming into the house. I was nervous and frightened and I couldn't talk. I used to go to my room and wanted to be left alone.

Even when my dear old friend, Mrs Molly Anderson, said she wanted to see me I said, 'No. I don't want to see Molly.' It was awful. They had to slowly lure me out of my room. People had to be calm, to help me to accept them. It was the most terrible feeling, suddenly being afraid of everyone, even your good friends.

I went to counselling at Darwin Hospital for about three or four months. The doctors had lots of people going through breakdowns after the cyclone. You'd talk and talk, telling your story, your history, and they'd listen to you. It was good therapy that, having somebody listen and take an interest in you. You can start to feel better when somebody shows you compassion.

It was a pretty rough patch there with all the sadness, fear and anger I'd never tried to face. Many Darwin people received counselling for three or four months. This made me feel in less of a panic, but deep down the bad feelings were still hidden. I'd never talked about the whole thing before, about the cyclone and Bill and all that. Bill had been my life from when I was sixteen, for nearly forty years. It took me a long time to be stable after that. It took a long time for the sadness and fear to fade into the past.

I just want to backtrack a little bit now. Over the Easter break in 1973, only a few months before Billy Muir was killed, I went to stay with my daughter Jeanie, and her new husband, David Chalmers, in Alice Springs. David found out that I hadn't been back to Borroloola since 1928. He had a good idea about driving up there and finding my family. So we drove up across the tableland. He was a good driver and he was pretty good at building fires, too. He'd gather the wood and Jeanie and I would try to stack it up to light it but it wouldn't burn. So David would knock it down and do it his own way.

When we got there we went to the Borroloola police station to ask about things. The same way my old Mum used to do. There was dear old Kathy O'Keefe, John Moriarty's mother, looking after the place. There was no house there then and the policeman lived in a caravan. Kathy said he'd gone off fishing. I introduced myself as Jarman and she give me a bit of a hug and told me my mother had died a few years before, but that my sister Jessie and my niece, Ivy were still living in a bit of a shack over by Rocky Creek. Kathy was pleased to see me and she took us across to Rocky Creek. There were some camps over that side, near the springs. There was no bridge, so we went across the creek. They had their camps over this side of the river. In my time, the old camps were over the other side. Some of them were still camped over there. The other mob, not Jessie. We didn't get over that side, so we just went along the river, Jeanie and I, and did some fishing. I don't remember what David was doing, probably looking around the town.

Anyway, Kathy told us to go over to Rocky Creek and we found the spring where there used to be a slaughter house and old Charlie Havey's house and shop. It was all gone and now there was just bushes and grass, instead. It was all overgrown, as if nothing good had ever been there. It was a real shock to me to see it like that. We were only there two or three days and then we had to leave. All this made me very sad. It seemed like there was nothing much left to go back to Borroloola for now. My mother was gone and I could speak only English; all my Yanyuwa language was gone. It's hard to talk to relatives and people who only speak their own language. I could only go back for a visit with a few relatives, or to show my children where their mother came from. It was very important to me, though, to show them my country. It was their country too. It was good to go back to Borroloola to see my place again after all those years. It reminded me of my origins and my early life.

The good thing was that I met my sister Jessie and her daughter, Ivy. That was when Jessie had a bit of a humpy, a bush shelter. When I saw Jessie after all those years I still remembered her. When we saw one another we just cried. I hadn't seen her since I'd left with the police patrol in 1928 and they hadn't taken her because she was a full blood. I don't remember if Jessie was there when I left, but I remembered her quite well when I saw her again, forty-six years later. I remembered my Aboriginal brother, Henry, too. He was dead and gone by this time as he'd been older than Jessie.

Many people were dead by then, some only a few years before I got back to Borroloola. I reckon I went back a little bit too late. But when I got there those who were left all knew me and called me Jarman and we cried and hugged. They were really sad that I hadn't been there earlier. It was hard to talk with no language, but I remembered all the old places we used to roam. All my close family had gone, except for my sister Jessie and her daughter, Ivy.

When the 1973 Easter break finished Jeanie and David went back to Alice Springs and I went back to my Commonwealth Hostel work in Darwin. That was the finish of my first trip back to Borroloola.

After the cyclone, when my daughter Cecilia was studying at the Aboriginal Task Force in Adelaide, I became sick. Cecilia decided she wanted me in Adelaide to see what was going on. The Darwin Hospital Ward One doctor said it might be a good idea to go to Adelaide for a while where Cecilia had her children in the Cabra Convent boarding school.

When I first moved down to Adelaide, my nerves seemed okay. But then I started getting bad and became worse than I had been in Darwin. This time I went to the lowest, lowest point, where you feel like you're reaching the end point. Cecilia was going off to college each day and didn't like leaving me on my own.

She got Hannah Anderson, my old friend Molly Anderson's daughter, to keep an eye on me. Hannah had a little house near Cecilia, so Cecilia asked Hannah if I could stay with her because she was there all the time. I was pretty bad, taking lots of tablets and Hannah had a job to watch me. She used to follow me round, thinking I might overdose, or get mixed up about what tablets I was supposed to take and when.

Gradually I must have been getting a little better and so having Hannah following and watching me was making me wild. I said, 'Hannah. I've noticed you watching me, following me every place. You're following me everywhere. What for? I don't like it.'

She said, 'Oh Aunty, I don't want to hurt you or anything, but I'm worried about you. We're worried you might take too much medicine.'

I said, 'No, Hannah, I know what I'm doing. I still know when to take my pills. I know how many to take.'

'Well, all right,' she said. 'But I'm only looking after you for Cissie. She wants me to look after you and that's all I'm concerned about.'

'No. I'm all right, dear. I know what I'm doing.'

But really I wasn't sleeping at night and I hated being there in the dark by myself. So I'd wake people up to get a light on and talk to someone.

Then Cecilia decided I should see the doctor in Goodwood. He was a Polish fellow, a nice chap who recommended I see a psychiatrist for trauma counselling at Hillcrest Hospital. I heard him say 'psychiatrist' and I told him I didn't think that I'd gone mad or anything.

In the end I must have agreed. I went to see the doctor at Hillcrest and when I got to the ward I saw funny-looking people. I tell you, it gave me a fright. 'I couldn't be that bad,' I said to myself, 'I'm not coming here. I'm not going in.'

It shook me up. I agreed to be a day patient, and go for counselling twice a week. It was the same as Darwin: just talk, talk, talk, and things from my early days. They just listened. I was getting things off my chest, getting things out.

I was starting to come right and there was a young fellow who used to go to Cecilia's place who said, 'I'd like to take Aunty to meditation.' He'd been on drugs previously, and was in bad shape. He took me to a place in Norwood that helped me a lot, it really built me up. I used to feel good and refreshed. He called it

Transcendental Meditation. I don't know if they've still got it there but that young fellow has gone on. He's a teacher now over in a big centre in Sydney.

Later I was invited to a place where you had to pay a lot of money. I said I was getting better, couldn't afford it and so I gave it away. But that Transcendental Meditation really fixed me up. I'll always be grateful to that young fellow. I know it was the Meditation that brought me around. I can still meditate now when I get upset. It's a very handy, good thing to know about and it's always there if you need it. It helps you control your mind and your fear.

It was a very rough patch there for more than a year. For two years I'd never talked about the cyclone or Bill being killed or being taken from my mother and losing my language. The thoughts were still there, though.

13

Hilda — World traveller

After my Fairstar cruise which I paid from my wages, the money for my travel came mostly from compensation for Bill's death in the cyclone. I reckon I got $10,000 for Bill being the breadwinner. Then there was what was left from his life insurance. Bill had started paying for life insurance in 1952 and he insured both of us. It was a high premium and he was paying a third of his wages which is why, later on, if he was short of money, he borrowed from his policy. Bill's policy was for $20,000 but, because he borrowed from his payout, the value had gone down. I cashed mine in and got about $6,000 which seemed like really big money to me. Then there was his final work pay-out, my money from working and both our holiday pays, long service leave and all that.

That's what gave me enough money to travel and see the world. I used to think of myself as an orphan girl who'd come from nothing and now had a bit of money and this was her time to see the world. And I blew it. I blew it all. I just went travelling for five years. I don't know, maybe seeing new places and meeting new people helped in my therapy. Those five years gave me the time to understand what sort of life I was going to have in the future. I was only fifty-four, nearly fifty-five, when my life was blown away and nearly forty of those years had been spent looking after Bill and our kids.

Bill didn't leave a will, so the children could have had all his estate, but they were great and they signed it all over to me. They could have been mean and greedy, but no, they knew I'd stuck with my husband through thick and thin. That I'd had bad times and good times, but that I'd stuck it out. I gave them all $1,000 each and they were happy.

It must have been in mid-1977 that I left Adelaide and went back to Darwin. That's when Isabel told me about a trip to America. 'Mum,' she said, 'Aunty Daisy says they're going to America for a couple of weeks. There's one vacant seat. Aunty Daisy asked me if you'd like to go on that trip. She said you must book right now.' We were to be VIP guests , promoting tourism for Aboriginal people. So I booked a seat straight away on the Grannie's Flight to America on 10 October 1977.

Not long after we took off in the plane I felt claustrophobic, as if everything was closing in on me. I felt very hot all of a sudden and I was pulling off my jumper and things. Somebody said, 'Hey you can't carry on like that, getting undressed.' But I said, 'I feel hot. I just want to take some of my clothes off.' They got the stewardess and she gave me oxygen and a cool drink and the oxygen seemed to settle me. Then we were invited up to the Captain's lounge and we met the pilot and his officers because we were special guests, VIPs.

There was only one stop on the way. You had to go through Customs in Honolulu and, I tell you, those Customs men looked like real gangsters. They looked tough and they treated us as if we were criminals. It wasn't very nice for Aboriginal grannies from Darwin to be treated in this way.

We arrived in California and booked into a top-class hotel, the Beverley Hills. We were several stories up and I looked out of the window and went all funny again. I said, 'I can't stand it. I can't stand all this top-class stuff.'

Daisy Ruddick came up and she said, 'Don't be silly now, Hilda. You've come all this way and you've paid all that money. Get hold of yourself and don't be silly. Pull yourself together!' Poor old Daisy gave me a big heart-to-heart talk and I settled down a bit, but inside it felt like I just couldn't cope.

The next day we toured Hollywood. That was something, I tell you. We saw where all the famous film stars put their handprints on the footpath and then at the Universal studio they showed us how they make films indoors — maybe even some of the cowboy films we saw at the Star Theatre in Darwin when we were in the Kahlin Home. Truly amazing. It was all a big eye-opener for a mob of Aboriginal grannies from Darwin. From there we went to the Anaheim Hotel, next door to Disneyland, where we stayed for three or four days.

My favourite thing in Disneyland was touring inside a small world on a boat. People of all nations — all dolls — were doing their national dance and singing It's a Small, Small World. The last place you come to is a poor old Aboriginal with his spear and a kangaroo, wallaby and emu. A poor old Aboriginal is the last man, the true Australian.

Then we toured by bus to Las Vegas. We had a look at the French Follies and it was lovely with all those beautiful girls in their feathered costumes with their long legs, kicking in time.

There was an Australian couple there who were touring around in a caravan. The place was full and they had a small child with them and badly wanted to sit down and see the show for the night. The waiter came over to see if we could put up another two and their little one. We said, 'Oh yes.' When the Australians met us they were really pleased to be with the Darwin grannies and their grandchildren, their own Australian countrywomen.

We went to a beautiful old mountain, Yosemite. The road is just on the edge of the mountain and we went round and around until we got down to the valley floor. Yosemite National Park has the thickest trees in America, so thick that cars can drive through the middle, which is carved out like a tunnel. There were big red trees they call Sequoia. The mountains were the highlight, though. People climb them and through binoculars we could see the climbers who slept halfway up. We couldn't believe it; it seemed really dangerous to us.

That night as the coach pulled in lots of furry animals came racing out, waiting for us to open the door so they could run in. Racoons. We came into the room and they were waiting for us to open our suitcases. That was a highlight, those beautiful, trusting animals all rushing in to see what we had for them.

There's another part of Yosemite National Park, a place called Muir's Wood. The sign there said 'Welcome to Muir's Wood.' I was sad that no-one took a photo of me standing under the sign, but I made a speech there, just for the fun of it. I was proud to be in Muir's Wood National Park.

Yosemite National Park was saved by a man called John Muir, a Scotsman. Yosemite is in what they call Indian country and he was an advocate for the Native American Indians when lots of people wanted to buy land, move in and build houses and towns. But John Muir wanted it kept as a national park and he won. It's now a big park with a trail there so you can walk around it.

We went back to San Francisco and although we didn't go to Alcatraz Island where they used to put the convicts, we went right up to the top lookout of the Golden Gate Bridge. You wouldn't believe it, but that morning the smog was so heavy that you couldn't see the city. Later, when it lifted, we went across the bridge and visited Chinatown which was huge — much bigger than Darwin's Chinatown.

After that we all did some shopping and then it was time to come home. This time on the plane I was fine and kept all my clothes on. Daisy and the others were relieved, and so was I. It was horrible to feel the way I had on the way over.

When I got back from the overseas trip my family told me that my sister Jessie was gone. She was up in Gove when she became ill, just before I'd left on my trip. Her son was working at Tennant

Creek, drinking heavily, and he died of an accident or a heart attack. Jessie took it hard. She died of a heart attack or a broken heart or something. So I missed her funeral too, and didn't have a chance to say goodbye and just after I'd found her again.

I felt great when I got back from my American trip, but after a while I seemed to drift back into depression and dark spirits again. Maybe it was knowing that Jessie was dead too, and that I really was alone now. I had no close Borroloola family left. Soon I found myself with a lot of other people, back for day therapy in Ward One at the Darwin hospital. It took me a long time to get myself straight again and in that time my mind was a jumble. Back in Darwin I seemed to be faced with reshaping my life all over again and it was very threatening to try to find who my real self was.

It seemed like I'd never had any time since I'd left Kahlin to find out who I was. No sooner had I got a job outside the Home than I'd met Billy Muir and fallen for him. Then he went to gaol and I went to Katherine. We had babies, got married, and then had more babies. Then the War came and Bill went off as a soldier and the babies and I went to Brisbane for four years. Then I grew up, and found out about real city life away from Darwin. Bill came back from War and told me to come back to Darwin and then I was isolated in homes I resented, still having babies, and losing one before he was even a year old.

Finally we'd got our War Service home and the children had all grown up and moved away. Then, just as Bill and I were really settling down, like old Darby and Joan, the cyclone came and took Bill away, as well as the house and all our possessions. Again I was evacuated to Brisbane where, thirty three years before, I'd started to learn about life.

Now I was back in Darwin, alone, with only dark spirits and sad thoughts for company and my nerves really let go. After more therapy I started to feel strong again and was itching to do more travelling. I still had a bit of money left, so I decided to get out of Darwin and see more of the world.

In the middle of 1980 I saw that the Fairstar was coming to Darwin again. My first trip on the ship had been good and so I booked another tour, this time to Manila, Hong Kong, Singapore and Bali. The Sitmar Line were so pleased that I'd picked them for a second cruise.

Manila seemed like a very noisy, dirty town to me and as we left we had to swing 50 miles off course to get away from the centre of a storm in the China Sea. It was quite scary for a bit with the high winds and waves. This storm was actually a typhoon.

I thought Hong Kong was really scary, so three or four of us stuck close to each other. Such tall buildings and so many people. One lady from Sydney took charge and she bargained for us when we went shopping. I was glad to do a bit of shopping and get back to the ship. The streets were so narrow I was glad to get home to Darwin, where I could breathe the air and see the sky overhead.

This tour wasn't as much fun as my first Pacific tour, although I still enjoyed being waited on in the dining room with the white tablecloths and silver. It was much better than crawling through the fence to steal scraps from the white's rubbish bins. Bali was lovely too — so different from Manila and Hong Kong.

When I came back I found my daughter-in-law, Christine, James' ex-wife, had been in touch with me. She had worked for Mrs Dawn Laurie, a Member of the Northern Territory Legislative Council, but now she was in England. I was getting itchy again for more travel so when Christine suggested I go to England to be with her, I said yes, and flew to London in September.

Father Frank Brennan and three other church people were on that plane, going to a conference in Rome, and there was a young girl going to Ireland to become a nun. They all looked after me as if they thought I needed a friend, especially Father Brennan. He was wonderful to me. He's a very gentle man who really cares about Aboriginal people.

Christine met me at the airport. We saw so much in London. The first trip was to Buckingham Palace and the Changing of the

Guard. I stared at where Queen Victoria used to live, the English Queen whose birthday the kids from the Kahlin Home celebrated with picnics on Mindil Beach. We went to Madame Tussaud's, the Tower of London and the House of Lords.

At Westminster Abbey I felt the spirit of God. The Chaplain asked us to join them in Evensong so we joined in singing all the hymns I love. To hear all the rich sounds of the voices in that big church was wonderful. It had a sort of healing power. We saw where the Archbishop of Canterbury had stood when the Queen was crowned and I could hardly believe that this little bush girl was really there, looking at it all.

I didn't want to miss anything and said, 'Yes, too right,' when Christine suggested we go to see the Farnborough air display. Christine took a photograph of the Concorde landing, coming in over my head. We also saw the Harrier jets, those red jump-jets. They'd be a good plane for the Flying Doctor I reckon — they can land anywhere.

Christine pampered me and I was like a mother to her. She used to call me 'Mum'. We did lots together and even went to a Tommy Steele concert where they called out 'Christine and Hilda Muir, from down under in Australia,' and of course we went to Trafalgar Square and fed the pigeons.

Then my girl said, 'We'll go to Scotland, there's a festival on.' It was the Edinburgh Military Tattoo and we went to the Highland Games and it was terrific. The Tattoo was the greatest show I'd ever seen. We were sitting on high platforms around a big open square and it was wonderful, especially when the pipers came marching in with their kilts all swinging, up to the last, single piper, up on the battlements. It was dark with a light just on him. I tell you, I wanted to cry. I really loved the bagpipes. Now, back home in Darwin, I always watch the Edinburgh Tattoo on television.

The trip to England and Scotland was my favourite. We saw so much and it was exciting seeing places I'd heard and read about for so long. Christine was thoughtful and kind, making sure I saw the important things and we stayed in the best places. Of all the places I've been, London is still my favourite. There's so much to do and see.

When I returned to Darwin I felt really good. It was as if all my black spirits had gone, as well as my awful depression. But still I was really sad that I'd only seen my old sister Jessie that one time at Borroloola in Easter 1973. There was so much more I wanted to ask her. But I was still itching to travel again and there was just one last place to go and see — New Zealand. I ran into Biddy Sallik and I told her I was going to New Zealand and she asked, 'Do you want me to come with you?' I said, 'Oh. If you want to, come.'

When I got to Brisbane airport where we were leaving from, Biddy was there looking really serious. She said, 'You know, we mightn't go on this trip to New Zealand.' It was a problem with names. In Darwin she'd booked as Mrs Sallik but in Brisbane she'd said Mrs Bin-Sallik. The man at the counter told her, 'Well, lady. If you want to go on this trip you either go as Mrs Sallik or you don't go.' She was really cranky about it, you know.

We finally flew off to Christchurch. People were coming from all over: the UK, Germany, Alaska, Malaysia, Japan and Victoria to join us on a fifteen-day coach tour. Biddy and I had a good look around Christchurch which is a pretty town, with really old buildings.

We went across to Mount Cook, in the Southern Alps which is where Sir Edmund Hillary trained before he climbed Mt Everest. The Tasman Glacier is near there and they reckon it's bigger than anything in Switzerland. In the Lake district there's a Maori legend about the evil spirit, Te Tipua, who eats people. The local people were sick of him, so one night when he was sleeping, the people covered him with bracken and bits of wood and set him alight. When the fire burnt him, he pulled his knees up, making the lake the shape it is. The hole burnt in the ground is called Whaka Tipu, which means 'the hollow of the giant'. They reckon they didn't burn his heart and that's why the lake sometimes rises and falls about three inches, every five minutes. Even the white scientists haven't got a better reason for why the lake 'breathes'. Maybe the Maori are right.

Next we went to the Te Anua area which is popular with bird watchers. The bus driver told us strange birds live there and make weird noises. Some bark like puppies and the kiwi, when it's frightened, makes a noise like a cat. That's where the Kakapo parrot, which is nearly extinct, lives in the rain forest. It comes out at night and can't fly, but it climbs trees and can glide.

Then we went to Milford Sound. One year, along a place called Disappearing Mountain Avenue, they had a 300 miles per hour whirlwind go through. That's much stronger than Cyclone Tracy so I'm glad it wasn't windy when we went or it might have given me another panic attack.

Milford Sound is just amazing. The water is very still and black and just looking at it makes you wonder how deep it is, and what's in there. Mitre Peak, the highest sea cliffs in the world, go up for a mile, and then extend 1800 feet under water. Near the water, along the edge of the cliffs, little fur seals were lying; the survivors of their ancestors who were nearly hunted to death during the early settlement times. I was sad when I heard this. I sort of knew how it must have been, getting hunted like that.

The bus went to Balfour and Riversdale and to Gore and I thought about my dear old brother, Harry Gore. Dunedin looked like Edinburgh and I told Biddy I'd seen the originals and I thought the Scottish people who went to New Zealand didn't have much imagination. I told her that I thought the real Edinburgh was better. She got cross then and told me I was showing off.

We crossed the Waitaki River and went to Timaru where Phar Lap came from. I was really thrilled to know that, because I love horse racing. The high hills all round Timaru protect that little town from the bad southerly storms blowing from the southern alps. I bet it's freezing there in winter.

At the airport, ready to go to the North Island, we got a shock to see a sign giving the departure and arrival times for planes to Antarctica. You'd never think about going to a place like that!

We went through the centre of the North Island and drove along Lake Taupo. This is where they have trout farms and people come from all over to fish for rainbow and brown trout. They reckon two tons of trout are pulled out of that lake every day, but that sounds like a real fishing story to me.

The bus stopped at Huka Falls and we drove down through the Wairakei Valley where you could see a whole valley spouting steam. The Maori say some of those steam holes have been on the boil for 600 years. From a distance the steam looked like bushfires to us Australians.

Rotorua, the centre of New Zealand's thermal springs, is a big centre for Maori culture. At the hotel, Maori put on hangi for us, and welcomed us to their country. I think Aboriginal people should do that when strangers and tourists come to their country, show them that we are still the owners, are still there in our country. That we still have our culture. We went walking over the boiling mud and they boiled a billy for us. I'd never seen or done anything like that, before. But the smell — sulphorous — oh!

Next we headed for Auckland. The driver said Ngaruawahia was where big Maori – European wars were fought a hundred years ago. Apparently lots of the soldiers fighting against the Maori came from Australia. Maybe they came over after they were stopped from shooting Aboriginal people in Australia. Auckland was full of Pacific Island people. It's the biggest mob of Polynesian people in any city anywhere.

So that was New Zealand. We landed in Darwin and I went to my daughter Jean and son-in-law David Chalmers's place. Cecilia was there, too, and other members of the family. And that was the end of my world travel.

Back in Darwin I got a little place to live in at Kuringal Flats at Fanny Bay. It was nothing too flash, but it was comfortable and close to the city and very solid. It would not blow away because it stood up to Cyclone Tracy. There were big trees and gardens around, a place to park cars and I was happy there. My people were living around me and popped in to see me quite often. I bet a little on the TAB, played a bit of Lotto and went visiting. On Sunday mornings I went to the AIM church.

I still got around too. I went over to Borroloola and one of my kids took me on trips when they were going anywhere. For example, I went down to Katherine and saw dear old Lindy Peckham. She was a special old lady, you know. A real old timer, that one.

Every Christmas I try to take a trip south to Adelaide, to get away from the cyclone season in Darwin. I stay with Cecilia and see her daughters, Maria and Franchesca, and all my great-grandchildren down there. Franchesca's got a good job at the Museum; she's a curator in the Anthropology section. She got a degree with Aboriginal Task Force and wants to go to Oxford to get a Masters degree. Her oldest child, Maria, is married to Andrew Wilson, and they've got five kids. Andrew works with State Archives, the records of the South Australian government. He's written guides for Aboriginal people so that they can find out about records held there about their families. He made an index of thousands of names in government records from 1836 to the present so that Aboriginal people can find out about ancestors.

Maria was a good mother — always happy and laughing. They had a lovely big old house and garden called a villa so I liked to go down and visit them each Christmas time. Maybe I've still got itchy feet after all these years.

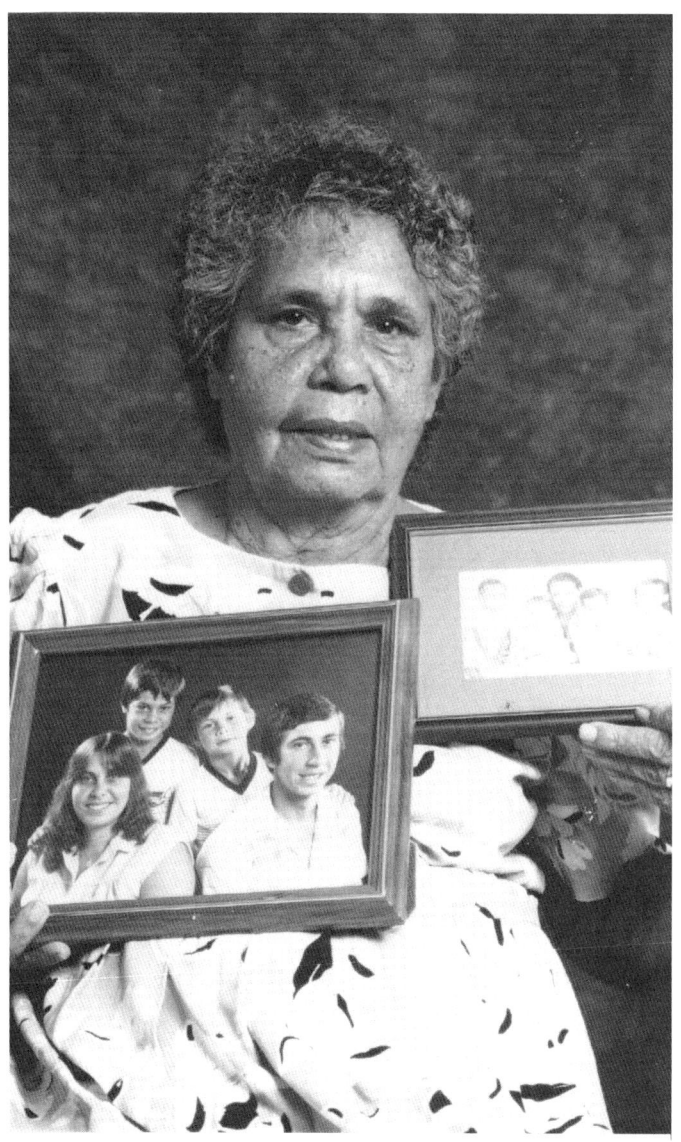

Hilda Muir, a proud mother, grandmother and great-grandmother.

Hilda's son Harold (now deceased) with sons (*left to right*) Dion, Tony and Harry, early 1990s.

Hilda with great-grandson Zac and (*standing left to right*) Nikki, Jordyn and Carole.

Harold's daughter Beryl, with her daughters (*left to right*) Danielle, Jodie and Marney.

Harold's son Tony and his wife Nikki and son Zac, 1999.

Harold's son Dion with his wife Petrice.

Hilda's son Tom with partner Shirley, 2003.

Son, Ali Muir, 2003.

Son, Billy Muir Jnr, 2000.   Jordan, Jessica and Jacob, Raymond and Cherie's children.

Billy Muir Jnr's son Raymond (Hilda's grandson) with his wife Cherie and children, 2000.

Grand-daughter Bianca (Billy Muir Jnr's daughter) with Hilda, 1998.

Sarah and Jaylene, Bianca's daughters and Hilda's great-grandchildren, 1991.

Hilda with son Robert (now deceased) with his granddaughter, Jessica, at her christening, 1990.

Robert's daughter, Mandy and family (*left to right*) Gale Rotumah, Tony (partner), Travis, Jessica and Mandy, 2000.

Grand-daugher Shelley (Robert's daugher) with Hilda, 2000.

Daughter Jean with son Alex and grandson Macson with Hilda, 2003.

Jean's daugher Sam, 2000.

Hilda's grandson Gordon and his wife Liz.

Hilda's daughter Cecilia, 2000.

Cecilia's daughter Franchesca with her baby niece, 1998.

Grand-daughter Maria (*left, backrow*) with Tarni, husband Andrew and (*sitting left to right*) Kira, Nara, Leui and Marley, 2003.

Grand-daughter Franchesca's children with cousin Kira (*left to right*) James and Jarda, 1990.

Celicia's daugher Inez (*second from left*) with her daughters (*left to right*) Tamika, Tana and Rokia, 2003.

Petra (*on right*), Cecilia's daughter, with Tamika (*far left*) and Hilda, and her children (*left to right*) Heather, Kimberley and Renee, 2001.

Son James, 2003.   James' wife Denise, 2003.

James' son, Ryan, 2000.   James' son Darren with partner Angela and son Mitchell, 1996.

Daughter Isabel (Muki) with partner Ross (Ski), 1995.

Isabel's son Brenton and partner Trudy, 2002.

Hilda with her grandchildren at her eightieth birthday party, 2000.

Hilda (*seated, centre*) with members of her family, 2003.

14

Time for change, right now

In October 1994 there was a big get-together in Darwin for people from the stolen generations. Karu, the Darwin Aboriginal Childcare Agency, organised a conference, mostly at the initiative of Barbara Cummings. Karu is funded by the Northern Territory Government and was set up after the 1983 Child Welfare Act came in. This new Act gave real powers to Karu and looked at the Aboriginal child placement principle. The purpose of the Act is to make sure that Aboriginal children are looked after by their own, and not put all over the place in homes, or with white foster parents as had happened for all those years. Aboriginal children must stay with their kin, even if it's just their extended families.

Karu also put children in touch with the Link-Up programs. This helped people who were taken away to find out who they were and where their families lived. Some of us were grandparents by this time, some even great-grandparents. We were part of the thousands removed under the old government policies. I know I'm a Yanyuwa person from Borroloola, so I'm okay.

Pretty soon people from the old institutions started to ask about compensation for being taken away. These people were now being called the stolen generations. Karu asked the North Australian Aboriginal Legal Aid Service (NAALAS) to help with a public meeting for all the stolen people and for help with legal advice. They used Barbara Cummings' book, *Take this Child*, written from interviews with people brought up in old Kahlin Home and the new home, Retta Dixon Home.

Karu organised the conference so that we could talk about what we wanted to happen under Link-Up. The main things we wanted were to find out how to get hold of the old archival material records, and our rights to land, compensation and social justice. Perhaps even to ask what happened to our money in the trust fund!

Karu held the conference during the International Year of the Family. There was also the opening of the Northern Territory Adoptions Register to help people trace their kin and country. They called it the 'Going Home' Conference. They got in touch with people who had been placed in various institutions. Representatives came from Garden Point, Croker Island, Retta Dixon, Groote Eylandt, and the Kahlin Compound, all Top-End places attended the meeting. While institutions from the Centre had groups from Bungalow, St Mary's and St John's, and people came from the other states too.

For the first time the stolen people were going to speak about what happened and how it's not right that we are still ignored by Australian history. Six hundred people got together: families, husbands, wives and children. All were also living away from their country, or not knowing where their country was, because their parents had been taken away when they were little kids. This was most important for us, that new generations of Aboriginal people didn't have rights to their country because their parents and grandparents had been taken away. Many didn't know what country they belonged to because no proper records had been kept. But white people didn't seem to care. Not even now. They act as if they don't understand what they did to us.

This is a big part of the reason I decided to tell my story. It's important for my future generations to know who they are and where they come from. To be proud of their Aboriginal heritage and to be strong for their country. The little ones living in Adelaide should know that their grandmother was a proud Yanyuwa woman from Manangoora, a saltwater woman. They should learn how their grandmother lived as a little bush girl with her mother, their great-grandmother, Manankurrmara, a big woman for her country. And that Nanna Hilda would have been a big woman for that country too if the police hadn't taken her away.

Now the younger generation only seem to know about watching TV and going to the corner shop.

But we don't just want compensation from the government. What we're really asking for is the recognition of our Aboriginal rights, our entitlement to be Aboriginal citizens of Australia. Not the big welfare stuff again. We've done that for too many years. We want to get recognition as Aboriginal people, officially. Not to be 'coloured' or 'half-caste', as if our mob's different from everyone else, even our kin. We want the government to agree that we're all Aboriginal, not some big problem in their way as they thought we were all those years ago. It's time for change, right now. For us to be called Aboriginal and not all those other names they gave us. We've got pride in our Aboriginal culture, as we always had. Now we want the name back.

The big experiment has gone on for too long. Now we want a say in who we are, and to be written into Australian history as part of the whole Aboriginal population and not to be known as just the problem people.

This is not just for the stolen people of the Northern Territory but for every Aboriginal person across the whole country. It's time they stopped saying what we are and let us decide for ourselves. In 1967 we were recognised as citizens of this country. Now it's time we had the right to be recognised for what we are. This Hilda is a Yanyuwa woman, born in Manangoora, near the Gulf of

Carpentaria. Except that the white authorities wanted me to be something else. The Yanyuwa people claim me for what I am and always have and know me as Jarman. The whites took me away and called me Rogers. All Yanyuwa people have our land waiting for us around Borroloola, McArthur River, Pellew Islands and the rest of that country. As they say, you can take the child out of Yanyuwa country, but you can't take Yanyuwa country out of this old woman.

At the Conference we were told by a lawyer from Melbourne, Mr Ron Merkel QC, that what the government did to us was illegal.

Mr Merkel was invited by the Katherine Aboriginal Legal Aid Service to tell us how we could go to the government and ask for justice. He told us that the government still had a responsibility for us and that it hadn't ended when they took us away and put us in institutions or fostered us out. After I left that half-caste home I had to make my own way, no-one ever helped me and I was often held up by government laws. I got some money and became a world traveller, seeing things I never thought I'd see. The government didn't help me with any of that.

The houses Bill and I lived in we paid for ourselves. Bill fought for his country overseas and he wasn't even recorded as a citizen until the referendum of 1967. Who was he fighting for, then? Not for himself and his half-caste lifestyle. Bill was a frontline fighter in New Guinea and he had malaria for the rest of his life. Because they couldn't stop him, he got a War Service Loan to build us a house at Fannie Bay and this was the first time we got a small hand from the government. But Bill had paid for that with his time in the Army.

And the government has never accounted for our Trust Fund monies, nor who got the benefit from them. The government even asked us to fund the preschool centre at Parap Camp. It looks like that's all the white government people are interested in: money. Not Aboriginal people and the way their white laws hurt us all, splitting up families and taking us from country, language and culture.

Mr Merkel told us that the federal government has an obligation to us still, even if they bring in laws now saying that the earlier times were different. They've still got to answer for why they haven't looked after their obligations.

The stolen generations are all getting old and it's a strain. Even those taken after 1957 are in their late thirties or early forties now, and those from Kahlin Home are about seventy years old. But they still call us 'stolen children'.

The Conference decided it was time to sue the federal government. The trouble was, the government wouldn't sit down and talk to us or let people tell them just what they did to us. The white way is to go through the law courts and this meant a big fight with white lawyers speaking for us, and us paying out lots of money. Even now the government is afraid to say sorry because that might mean they're admitting they were guilty of going against the law and would have to pay compensation. Ron Merkel reckoned the government wasn't looking at a moral right, only a legal one and that some of us from the stolen generations had to stand up and tell our story in court.

What we want to do is heal our pain and get some justice. To get the government to say that what they did was wrong but they kept making laws and telling us to fit in with them. So now we have to deal with whitefella law in three areas: the Land Rights Act, Sacred Sites Act and the Native Title Act. For people who were taken away from their country, there are problems doing things under the Sacred Sites Act. We have to say if we're the traditional owners and custodians, but if we have no language and don't know our country, how can we? It looks like their policies aren't much different now from the old days.

In April 1995 I was chosen as one of a group going to Melbourne to put a writ to the government in the High Court. We had to lodge the application with the Court. After talking with us for a long time Mr Ron Merkel QC wrote out our complaints against the government's actions, asking for damages for 'cultural, family and spiritual loss and suffering'. It said removing us 'breached the Australian constitution and the International Genocide Convention'. There was a lot of stuff in there I'm not too clear about now, but when we read it and talked about it we reckoned it covered what we felt we wanted put right.

Alec Kruger and I were the plaintiffs representing the stolen generations. I represented the Top-End kids, and Alec was there for the Alice Springs kids.

It was the most exhausting, exciting experience of my life. I had to keep pinching myself to see if it was real. What's happening to this bush girl, going to the High Court and representing all her people? Barbara Cummings, who wrote *Take This Child*, and was the founder of Karu, was our minder. Brian Butler was there, the Chairperson of the Secretariat for the National Aboriginal and Islander Child Care Agency (SNAICCA) and representing the Child Welfare Department. Then there was Wesley Miller, from the North Australian Aboriginal Legal Service (NAALS) and Vicki Nangala Tippett from Nangala Media in Darwin.

Melbourne was very cold after Darwin, so I had to borrow a thick coat to keep warm. A lovely red one, it was. We were all very nervous when we got to the High Court. It felt like a dream that a Kahlin kid was actually there, making a claim against the government for what they'd done to us. It was eerie, walking through the corridors of power in the High Court. The media were there harassing us, sticking microphones in our faces. Inside, one man, a journalist, thought he was allowed to be there, but he was told he wasn't.

When we came out and down the stairs in front of the press we hugged one another and cried as we released all our emotions. It was well done, and over. I felt really proud to have been chosen to represent my people from the Top-End, and from the rest of Australia. It's an opening for others to follow.

I've got really mixed feelings about what happened to me in my life. These are not anyone else's feelings but mine. I feel no bitterness, but sometimes my emotions get the better of me. This is the way I look at it…back then the authorities thought they were doing what was best for us. They probably had good intentions. You can't believe anyone would just do that to little kids and their mothers for bad reasons, to be really cruel. It was policy — the law, and for our welfare. If you think they did it for bad reasons, you go a bit crazy.

Maybe I would have liked to live out in the bush and be happy roaming with my people. But then I wouldn't have met Billy Muir, had all my children and travelled the world. But perhaps if I'd stayed I might have met someone else, someone living round Borroloola, and then I could have kept and eye on my country. I would have had my old Mum and a lot of other things that were important to me.

You have to weigh it all up. When they took us, everything had to be forgotten, just left behind — culture, people, language. I still always regret that I was never able to go back to see my people, especially my mother. It seemed like it was always just too hard and too far to go all that way until Jeanie and David took me there in 1973.

I had family, all those kids to care for, and homes to look after. When I went back in 1973 I met my half-sister Jessie and we had a great reunion and hugged and cried together. I was happy to see someone I still remembered — my mother's other daughter, my sister. She told me my dear old mother had died.

I was happy to be one of the party lodging the writ because I wanted some respect and recognition for my culture. We weren't asking for anything big, just the recognition that what had been done was wrong. I'm not the sort of person to hold a grudge or ill-feeling. I'm a happy person, really, but when I think about it all, I still get choked up with emotion.

As you get older, you crave closer connection with your own and this is what is still denied us. Maybe if the government could say sorry, that they were wrong all those years ago, we could say okay, you got it wrong. It was bad what happened to us, but if you're sorry, then we can say thank you.

My view is that all this talk about big compensation is in the mind of the government and the lawyers. Maybe because money is so important to whitefellas they think that's what we're saying. Of course compensation is something sought by some groups. But compensation is not going to bring back time with my mother, give me back my language and my culture, or put me back as a bush child roaming over my country. I'm an old woman now, living in the city, going to church on Sundays, going to the TAB, playing Lotto, and shopping at the corner shop or at the Casuarina shopping centre. I've got children, grandchildren and great-grandchildren all over the place, some here in Darwin, some in Brisbane and some in Adelaide. But it would be good if the government could see how they hurt us, and say sorry. To say sorry and to recognise our culture and our right to speak our language. Not doing this means we're still treated like a problem, as not belonging; we could start to be free and get on with our lives without feeling angry and mixed up all the time. I think we only get cross because the government just doesn't see what we're on about, even now. They're afraid to sit down and talk, person to person. They're making us use their rules and then they always make sure we lose again.

I arrived back from Melbourne with a chest infection. I was really worn out with all the emotion. It had been a big strain. Then I had bad news about my son, Harold. He'd been living in Brisbane but when his marriage broke up he came back to his old home town and got a job in Darwin. Slowly his health started going downhill and the doctor told us he had lung cancer. After a while he wanted to be near his family so he went back to Brisbane and shared a house with a young bloke from Darwin. My son Harold died of lung cancer in May 1996.

We all went down for his funeral service and there was a lovely wake for him at the Manly Hotel where he used to drink. All his friends were there. Harold was a well-liked man who'd loved Brisbane ever since he was evacuated there as a small boy. One of Harold's sisters couldn't get to Brisbane, so she arranged a funeral service in Darwin at the same time as the Brisbane one. There were mobs of people at the Darwin service too and they held a big wake for him at Nightcliff Football Club where he used to play football. And that was just what Harold would have liked: everyone had plenty to drink, told stories and there was singing. Aboriginal wakes are quite cheerful affairs, people tell stories about the one that's gone and remembering all the good times. Good old Harold. He was a good son.

In July 1997 we heard that the High Court had thrown out our writ saying we didn't have the right to sue the government for being at fault. All we were claiming was that the laws they had used to steal us from our culture were not what the Constitution promised and that we should have a right to family. Most of the High Court judges disagreed with our claims, so we weren't successful. They reckon it all happened too long ago. The thing is that we were still hurting. Maybe what they'd done was a long time ago, but the effects were still with us. It seemed that the government people were just looking at their law books and using their heads, not their hearts.

There's no way they're going to give us justice, not even now. They just want us so-called yellafellas to shut up and take what they give. We've still all got to play the whitefellas game: lying to make them feel good.

But we all have other bits of our lives going on. Good bits, happy bits. I go out to Borroloola when I can, and I keep in touch with whoever's left there. I go to Adelaide in the cyclone season, see my kids and their kids down there. My grandson, Dion Muir, is a great sportsman, like his father Harold, playing cricket, rugby and other games. He was playing at the Indoor Cricket International, so I went down to Melbourne to see him play at Glasshouse and it was great. His team won, so we were all very happy and I was a really proud grandmother.

All these things give you a bit of interest in life, they keep you going. One thing I learnt in life is this: it's no good complaining.

You've just got to take what happens and make the most of it. And that's what I've done all my life, really. You mightn't always have what you think you might want, but there's no good kicking up about it.

I love all my children and their children and they all love me, Nanna Hilda, as do all the other kids from my sisters and brothers in the Kahlin half-caste Home who call me Aunty. Looking back on my life, I reckon I've been a lucky woman to see so much, do so much, including travelling after I lost Billy. It's so amazing that I've seen so much of the world, visited so many interesting places, and met so many good people on my travels whom I keep in touch with and visit when I can.

But there was one more bit of bad news to come. I got a phone call saying that dear old sister Lindy Peckham was gone. She wasn't too well so they put her in hospital because the doctor wanted to do some tests. But Lindy wanted to go home because her card ladies were waiting for her. So she left hospital and went home to Katherine. She lived for her cards, you know — that bit of company. Her daughter came early in the morning to make sure she took her pills and found her. The doctor says she had a heart attack on Wednesday, 14 April 1999. So dear old Lindy, a foster child of Sarah and Jim Scully, died when she was about 96. That's the last of the old ones. She'd married Harry Peckham, the son of the Fizzer, the mailman in We of the Never Never. There was a big funeral for her and I feel sad that she's gone. It was lovely that she wasn't still in hospital. That's the best way to go, I reckon — a heart attack in your own house. She was Nanna Lindy to so many.

So that's the end of my story and if people want to say that's not what happened, then good luck to them. I've told my story, the good and the bad, as I remember it. I hope it helps my younger generations understand who their ancestors are and keeps them in touch with their country.

Maybe there's just one more adventure left for me. I'd really like to go back to my country and have a good look around those bits where we used to roam, hunting for food. Go out to Vanderlin Island. I could see if our friend John Bradley can take me and a few of my relatives out there, and see where we all were when Gilprey murdered my uncle and aunt; see if it jogs my memory.

15

Kidnapped back home

This chapter is written from the perspective of John Bradley, an anthropologist and a respected member of the Yanyuwa Aboriginal community who helped Hilda to return to country. Hilda's own comments are included throughout.

On a warm afternoon in June 1999 I stood at the Borroloola airstrip, waiting for a chartered aircraft to arrive from Darwin. Aboard the plane were Hilda Muir and her grandson Gordon Chalmers. I was at Borroloola acting as senior anthropologist for the Northern Land Council. We were documenting information about a land claim over a 160 kilometre stretch of coast in the Gulf of Carpentaria. Some of the country we were documenting was Hilda's mother's country. It was, as things turned out, to include country which Hilda would also call her own.

During this work, I found I had a 48-hour window of opportunity when it would be possible to take Hilda to Manangoora (Manankurra). This is her mother's country on the Wearyan River, some 100 kilometres to the east of Borroloola. Manangoora is a place which resonates with deep emotion for Hilda. It was a location she had long wished to visit, and a visit I had long said I would try to help her achieve. I also had a deep conviction that if the title 'anthropologist' was worth anything to Indigenous Australians, then it was meant for moments like this.

I had two other people with me, Dr Sarah Holcolme from the Northern Land Council, and Sailesh Rai, a lawyer. Both were keen to help Hilda get back to her mother's country and the land of her childhood. Before the plane arrived, we had gathered together some camping equipment and were now waiting, rather excited about what we were going to do.

The plane landed and a number of Yanyuwa people who live in Darwin came off the plane, along with Hilda and Gordon. At the same time, Hilda's daughter, Muki, pulled up and began to load her mother's gear into her vehicle. I suggested she put it into my vehicle and told Muki what we'd arranged as a surprise for her mother. Muki was a little taken aback but I explained to Hilda what I proposed to do, and that daylight would soon be gone, so I wanted to get moving. Within twenty minutes of the plane landing, we were on our way.

> I was expecting Muki, there to meet me – she went to Borroloola earlier by truck. But she was five minutes late, and John Bradley put my stuff in his truck. I thought all along our plan was to go to Fat Fellows Creek. I had no idea that John Bradley had all this in mind! It was wonderful! A lovely surprise. I wasn't game to travel to Manangoora, I used to think I couldn't make it all that hard way, but this time I didn't think.

The road was unsealed, and once onto the main Manangoora road it was very rough. Hilda was excited but also apprehensive. She was an old lady, and she had already had a long day flying from Darwin. However, she too could see what this window of opportunity represented. She said as we drove east 'It was either do it now, or I might die before I get another chance. I feel as though I have been kidnapped back home!' This was an interesting play on words given that members of what we now call the stolen generations, one could argue, were indeed kidnapped from their homes and family.

I had mentioned to other senior Yanyuwa men and women that I intended to take Hilda to Manangoora. All were keen to see it happen. As it turned out, however, health checks before going bush, travel to do with the land claim and other family commitments meant none of them could come along. We wouldn't have been able to fit anyone extra in the vehicle anyway. A number of these older people all mentioned that Hilda should be reintroduced to her mother's country. This is an important Yanyuwa custom and usually involves an oration (short or lengthy) to the country so it will know the person again.

One of Hilda's sisters — (in Aboriginal law) — Dinah Norman said to me, 'The old lady might be too choked up, you know, you want to be careful. You'd better talk for her.' This really came as a bit of a shock to me. After twenty years of working with Yanyuwa people I can speak Yanyuwa reasonably well and I am aware of the rules of etiquette when talking to country. Dinah immediately sensed my hesitation, and said, 'You know that place. My sister is old, we don't want something to go wrong.' She then added in a stern tone, 'We haven't taught you for nothing.' In Yanyuwa-speak, the 'something' Dinah was talking about could range from spiritual attack, illness, or in worst-case situations, death. People visiting country they have not been to for a long time can be at risk.

> John, he's a proper Yanyuwa man you know. They polished him to every detail of the law. He's really absorbed things, and will do the right thing by family. He was a young man when he went to Borroloola; a schoolteacher he was. I was always surprised he never married an Aboriginal girl, but no, he married one of his own.

The journey to Manangoora was now filled with other less tangible but no less important responsibilities. I spent most of that trip talking to Hilda about the country we passed through. Though interested, she was also anxious: how much further was it? Was the road rough? I began wondering if I had asked too much of Hilda. She was, after all, 79-years-old. I was concerned too that it was dusk and I desperately wanted to be there before nightfall so we could make camp, and so Hilda could see Manangoora and the Wearyan River at this most beautiful time of day. Dusk accentuates the beauty of the broad-sweeping bend of the river, its ochre-coloured eastern banks and the huge ancient cycad palms standing like sentinels along the river.

The last part of the journey was uncomfortable. The road was very rough and covered in sand ridges, corrugations and large holes full of bull dust. A few times Hilda told me to slow down, and rightly so. I was living up to my Yanyuwa nickname, Wirarra — the impatient one.

> I was thinking the distance was wrong. Because we used to go hunting from the camp, and I was thinking, oh, we didn't go this far…And rough! Absolutely up and down! Not just corrugated — proper potholes. It was very bad. Worse later on the boat though, slamming up and down into the waves. I thought, 'There can't be much wrong with my heart!' I was that shaken up, I had to rest for a couple of days when we got there.

We arrived with the sun still high enough not to worry so much, and went up to the station buildings on the river bank. Steven Anderson met us at the station. He's one of the older sons of Lenin Anderson, who was the son of a Swede and a local Garrawa Indigenous woman. I explained to him who we were, and the personal nature of the trip. He wasn't at all impressed, and began to argue that there were no traditional owners for country. As far as he was concerned it was his family's country, and they were working it. I felt Hilda's ire at this, and she demanded to know who this person was. He gave his name, and Hilda's mental gymnastics of family relationships between

Darwin, Borroloola and Manangoora took over. After a few well-placed comments about family, we had negotiated to stay downstream at a place used by Yanyuwa people when visiting. Hilda had been impressive. No-one was going to stand between her and her mother.

> No. I wasn't going to just think he could tell us to move on, or something. I was a bit angry! They had this high fence there — I don't know if people had been coming around and maybe he was protecting his family. He wasn't too happy. But I just went up and said it. He said okay then.

When we arrived, I stopped the car and Hilda got out and kissed the ground. She was 'home' after about 72 years. She had finally made it. I took Hilda by the hand and led her to the eastern bank of the river and I sang out in Yanyuwa:'Here she is, one whose mother came from this place, her mother was a-Manankurrmara and this is her child standing with me. She has been away for a long time but now she has come back and is crying for this country. Please do not ignore her, she was away but now she has returned. She is truly a kinswoman to this place.'

It was done. Hilda stood for a while on the banks of the river alone. She was lost, perhaps, in recall of the country that gave birth to the spirit of her mother.

> We had to face across the river. Talk to the spirit. That was an emotional thing. John's heart, it was there. Something just hard to describe, with all this emotion in me. It was just so beautiful... Something there. You belong. It was true, the spirit is there. You believe you are in your own world, and part of that country. I felt so strong afterwards, so rejuvenated. From that time I never looked back. I still feel that strength in me, that same way.

We put up the tents and had a barbecue. During this time Hilda told us that she could remember the cycad palms and the old people gathering and treating them before grinding, cooking and eating them. Her most vivid memory, though, was the sweeping high banks on the eastern bank of the river. She was sure that night that God had truly blessed her.

The next morning was a time of photos with her grandson Gordon, of quiet talks and short walks, of gathering some soil from Manangoora, some cycad nuts and a cycad frond. They were, as Hilda simply stated, 'for memory'. We packed up and waited for the boat to come and take us to Milrila, Fat Fellows Creek. This was where the first important meeting was going to take place between the Yanyuwa and Garrwa claimants, and their anthropologists, lawyer and barrister.

The next journey for Hilda was down the Wearyan River and from the river mouth east to the Creek — a distance of some 31 kilometres. The river was calm, and in the early morning light we were lost to our own thoughts. As a child Hilda would have travelled this same river in a dugout canoe. Now she had returned and was travelling it in a fifteen metre aluminium barge. When we got to the mouth of the river, the broad sweep of the Gulf lay before us. On the horizon was the low relief of the Pellew Islands. In the east the long, low mass of Vanderlin Island could be made out. It was, of course, events on this island that had led to Hilda's removal from mother, family and country.

Hilda found the sea journey hard and tiring. She hadn't really stopped. She'd travelled where she never thought she would, and had had to deal with emotions at many different levels. Of constant amazement to her were the distances between the mainland and the islands, which she had travelled in dugout canoes. The distances looked so vast. We talked for a while about her life on the island, and then lapsed into silence, broken only by the wind off the sea, and the steady drone of the boat's engines.

Our next landing was two kilometres up Fat Fellows Creek. The Northern Land Council has constructed a base camp there, with basic facilities. This has made camping on what is no more than a mangrove saltpan a little easier. Hilda spent much of her time here listening to claimants tell of their relationships to the land and sea under claim, fishing, and sitting at night with her family as they sang of the ancestors who once moved across the land. At night Hilda's profile could often be seen in the firelight as she danced to the lyrics sung by her sisters, cousin and other relatives.

> I feel in the mood, and I like to get up and join them. Even now in Darwin, if there's a bit of music I get up and put on an act, carry on silly. That's the mood I get into.

Two important events happened once we arrived at Fat Fellows Creek. The first was that Hilda was able to tell her own story to all her Yanyuwa relatives. Many of these had never heard it. It was a cool morning when about thirty men, women and children sat in a circle on the saltpan and Hilda began to talk. It was an emotional event. She talked of her memories of Manangoora, her young womanhood, of her joys, losses and gains. Of kind people and harsh treatment, of death and destruction during Cyclone Tracy and then of returning to Borroloola and her feelings for her mother and country.

Hilda spoke quietly, with authority and emotion about her life. She was supported both physically and emotionally throughout by Eileen McDinny, her kinswoman. After about an hour, she stopped. People were silent; many had tears in their eyes. She had returned to her own family and country and had at last told her story in as full a way as possible. Hilda left no-one in any doubt as to how she felt about her Yanyuwa identity and her country. True, she didn't know much about the law; her language and family had been taken from her by enforced institutionalisation. But she was from this place, and related to everyone there. As she said, 'It is my heart, this land, this family. It is my feeling nothing else is important.'

The next day Hilda travelled the eight kilometres across to Clarkson Point on the tip of Vanderlin Island. On arrival at Vanderlin, she once again kissed the ground. Another link in the jigsaw of her life had been reclaimed. She met Steve Johnston, a man of Yanyuwa and Scots descent, who had lived on the island all his life. Hilda asked him where the old wooden jetty was. Steve was a little taken aback by this old woman asking about things from before he was born. His initial suspicion evaporated; yes, it was true a jetty had once been where Hilda had said.

Steve later said, 'All my life I knew Hilda's mother, Old Polly a-Manankurrmara, and there she was, she came back after all those years. How's that? She found her way back. There's a lot of poor buggers never do, but she did, and I will tell you I was amazed. Her memory was clear, she still knew it all. It brought tears to my eyes.'

For Hilda each of these experiences was a confirmation of her story, of the events that had been part of her long life. They had shaped all that she now was, and was becoming. Each journey into the country of her ancestors brought more stories, new insights into how she fitted into both the land and the sea and her people who have always called it home. These new insights were not without emotional dilemmas. It sometimes seemed for Hilda to be a difficult learning.

The most telling example of this was in regard to Hilda's mother's country as her own true country. It was the one substantial link to her mother that no-one could take. Now, due to the dictates of the Land Rights Act (NT) 1976, Hilda had to define her rights to that land if she wanted recognition as its owner under European law. It wasn't enough to have been born from and into the land. She had to speak of her mother's Spirit Ancestors: The Tiger Shark, the White-Bellied Sea Eagle. She was expected to know more than she thought she could learn. Hilda did learn though, and with patient (and sometimes impatient) help of her Yanyuwa family and myself as hasty anthro and friend, we talked through the stories she was hearing.

I still wanted to hear more. I wanted to refresh my mind from the family. And they loved to talk about it, and go over it. They really got that. They've still got custom. The generation that came after me, they've still got that really deep religious respect for that tradition. I don't know about the young ones now. Maybe they're in the Western world now. In my time the old people would sit them down and teach them and they would listen. But I don't know now.

The other perplexing issue for Hilda was that she was told she owned country through patrilineal descent. This was a conundrum for Hilda, since her father was a white man. People explained that in Yanyuwa law she had to have country of her own. To do this, they told her of her stepfather who had married Polly when Hilda was small. This man was Wangkangkarramaliji; his country was on Kangaroo Island and the lower tidal reaches of the McArthur River and Crooked River. Hilda's own bush name, a-Kangkarrija, was from this country. Her own dreamings, her own Spirit Ancestors, were different from her mother's.

Hilda found some of this very hard. To be given different country and different Dreamings was a sort of separation from her mother that she'd never imagined. People were at pains to tell her that no-one could take Manangoora away from her, she still had important rights there. But Hilda had spent years with one name on her lips in relation to her mother, and that was Manangoora. Now, because of white law, it was all changed; it had to change if she was to be officially recognised as having any country at all.

After four days at Fat Fellows Creek, and a good many fish later, people began to leave by light aircraft charter. They met up again at Kangaroo Island, an island formed in the McArthur River delta by the two major branches of the McArthur River proper and the Carrington Channel. This is the country Hilda is associated with by paternal adoption.

We made many day trips in the following week, along all of the major river systems, to South West Island and to Sharkers Point off the mouth of the Crooked River. Hilda was to be found on all these journeys, with fishing line, bait and a cheerful face. A word common on her lips at this time was 'beautiful'. It seemed as if the country that should have nurtured her through her life was making up for lost time. Hilda listened to the stories of the others; she learned of all the possible threads of connection that existed between her and the land and her Yanyuwa family. At the end of the week she had been called Queen of the McArthur. She was now the oldest claimant, and fully determined to see the exhausting land claim process through till the end. With these thoughts and a wealth of memories, she returned to Darwin. In January 2000, Hilda celebrated her eightieth birthday.

Six months later, we once again all met on Kangaroo Island. There were two weeks of proofing the land claim documents before the claim proper was to be heard in front of Justice Olney, the Federal Land Commissioner. Hilda was ready for the final events of the arduous process that had already led her over many hundreds of kilometres of Gulf Country. Her daughter Muki and grandson Gordon were there as representatives of a large, scattered family.

Hilda camped with her relations whose mothers also came from Manangoora. As at Fat Fellows Creek, nights were spent around the fire singing, dancing, playing cards, telling stories and talking about the claim. Hilda spent her daylight hours listening to claimants tell stories of their land, their family connections, and why they were the owners. It was during this time that she learned her mother had died on her country at Manangoora but no-one knew the location of the grave.

> So I couldn't trace where dear old Mum was buried. Where she had been put to rest.

There were issues in the land claim that were about legitimacy and identity for Hilda. She had already been to court to argue for recognition and compensation for the victims of the stolen generations. Now she would be involved in a court case that would suggest to the judge that though she and her family who had come after had been dispossessed, they were still entitled to be land owners, and were recognised as such by Yanyuwa people who still lived and moved across the land.

During the days leading to the court case the weather was unseasonal. We had days of rain and biting south winds, rather than the normal warm days with cloudless blue skies. The savannah grass we camped on was soft and boggy, uncomfortable for all of us. Through all this Hilda maintained her sense of humour. 'What's a bit of rain?' she said. 'We're all well, and here to do an important thing.' For members of her family this unseasonal rain was Murnnyi, Winter Rain, a Dreaming Ancestor that someone had sung because they were jealous of the claim taking place on Kangaroo Island.

Justice Olney arrived on Kangaroo Island. With him was the then Minister for Aboriginal Affairs, John Herron, who had requested to view a land claim at first hand. The tension that morning was tangible. The Yanyuwa were still angry with Mr Herron because he had not officially returned land to them won in a previous claim in 1992. Hilda had other stories concerning lack of recognition by the Howard Government of the members of the stolen generation (or as she sometimes put it, the ones who were kidnapped).

> He called me Aunty Hilda, you know! Oh, I don't say people are two-faced. If they're nice to me, well…

On the morning the court opened it was bleakly grey weather, touched with light rain and a steady south wind. The court was officially opened by a group of senior Yanyuwa women singing Kalwanyarra, or Spirit Man. They came up from the river bank to singing provided by the men. There, amongst the dancers, painted in white ochre, was Hilda. At eighty years of age she was not only the oldest claimant, but also the oldest dancer in the group.

After a number of speeches the court convened, and this began ten days of hearings. Some of these took place in court and some took place on visits to the land and sea. Hilda was an ever-present entity in court, which was really no more than a big shady cloth tent. She had her own comments on what was happening, nodding her head in agreement as family told their stories, and growing angry if someone seemed too light-hearted or flippant.

The day came when the barrister from the Northern Territory Government asked her family who shared Manangoora as mother's country, if Hilda was really a traditional owner for the area. Her family replied, 'Yes, of course you are.' Hilda sat with quiet dignity as her family explained how not only she, but other members of her family such as Muki and Gordon had to be 'put back onto country'. Just because they lived away from Borroloola did not mean they could be excluded. As one of Hilda's younger relatives Nancy McDinny said, 'We've got a feeling for our family, they belong with us, and they belong on the land, you can't take that away.'

> I could hear them, that Annie Karrakayn was the loudest. And Dinah, too. They sang out in my defence.

On the day Hilda was cross-examined she explained her story quietly. Justice Olney listened with appreciation. Her story, by now familiar to many Australians, was still moving. She was now able, because of her families' teaching, to tell the judge she was a jungkayi, a guardian for her mother's country. She was also ngimarringki, an owner for Kangaroo Island, the Crooked River and the lower McArthur River. She told the judge she was still learning, and had a lot of catching up to do.

During her evidence Hilda submitted photographs of the family she had been with on Vanderlin Island at the time of the murder, and also of the murderer himself. These photos had been found by historian Tony Roberts who had realised their importance to Hilda and passed them on. She told the judge the names of the people in the photograph, and that they were her relatives. By the time the photos had been taken at the Borroloola Police Station, Hilda was not amongst her family. She was, as she said, 'Probably in the police house somewhere with the policeman's wife'. The people in the photo were the same group she was to travel to Darwin with for the murder case all those years ago.

Hilda mentioned to Justice Olney that she was writing a book about her life. He suggested he would like a copy when it came out. With a bright sparkle in her eye and without wavering, Hilda suggested that if His Honour saw fit to give her and her family's land back, she might give him a copy. It was humour at its best, and Justice Olney took it in good stead. Their exchange is recorded in the official court notes.

> I was just laughing up, a bit of humour. Not realising I could have been up for contempt of court!

I had first met Hilda when I was a much younger man. It was 1984 when she came into my office in Darwin when I was working for the Aboriginal Sacred Sites Protection Authority. She had come in to ask if I knew anything about her family. She told me her mother's name was Polly, and after a brief conversation, she left.

A few months after this initial meeting I had been able to give Hilda a copy of her family tree. As I now sat in court on Kangaroo Island in 2000, watching Hilda and her family give evidence, I remembered that time, and the time when, at Borroloola, I first drew up the family tree. I was working with an old lady, long since deceased. When I put Polly a-Manankurrmara's name down I asked if she had had any sons or daughters. 'Yeah,' the old lady said to me, 'One daughter, her name is Hilda. She's there somewhere in Darwin.'

Hilda still lives in Darwin today, but as she says, her heart is on the land of her mother and her people. I realised as I watched the court proceedings in 2000 that both of us had travelled a long way from that first meeting in my office. We still don't know what the judge will say, but Hilda has come home. She has told her story to the highest court in the land where such things matter. She has walked the land of her childhood again. She has travelled the sea, and seen the islands, and through it all she was strengthened, her spirit was renewed. She came home, and the land and the people had waited, and they remembered her.

Postscript — An apology

On the morning of 16 October 2001, members of the Northern Territory's Stolen Generations gathered at Parliament House in Darwin. The by now middle-aged and elderly children were there to hear an address by the Chief Minister, Clare Martin, only just recently elected.

Hilda, at the time 81, had had an important medical appointment that morning and anxiously waited for this to be completed at the Darwin Hospital. 'I have to be there by 10,' she told the nursing staff, but there were some delays and Hilda was unable to make it to the Assembly to take her seat in the Chamber. The seat reserved for Hilda was the one next to her Kahlin sister — Daisy Ruddick. The doors to the Chamber had been closed by the time Hilda arrived from the hospital, so Hilda watched Question Time in the foyer on a large television. At recess Hilda was able to enter the Chamber and take her seat in the Gallery. She was looking on as the Chief Minister delivered the Government's apology to the stolen children and their families.

Hilda commented afterwards — 'This is an apology that has been a long time coming. I don't know if it had to be a woman to do it. It's as if Clare's the only one who has the heart or something. She has that feeling. She knows what a mother's love is. She understands what it is to have a child taken from you.'

Conversion table

Imperial to metric equivalents follow:

one inch = 25.4mm
one foot = 30.5cm
one yard = 91.5cm
one mile = 1.61km
one ounce = 29.3g
one gallon = 4.6l
one acre = 0.405ha